America's Favorite Radio Station

America's Favorite Radio Station:

WKRP in Cincinnati

by

Michael B. Kassel

The University of Wisconsin Press

The University of Wisconsin Press
1930 Monroe Street, 3rd Floor
Madison, Wisconsin 53711-2059
uwpress.wisc.edu

3 Henrietta Street
London WC2E 8LU, England
eurospanbookstore.com

Printed in the United States of America

Library of Congress Catalogue Card No.: 93-70630

ISBN 978-0-87972-585-3 (pbk.: alk. paper)

To Larry,

the best brother a guy could have

Contents

Contents

Acknowledgements

Two and one-half years have passed since I first began researching and writing about *WKRP in Cincinnati*. During that time I have met or have become better acquainted with a number of wonderful people who have helped me with this project. The following people are proof that writing is much more than a solo performance.

I am greatly indebted to the West Coast *WKRP* alumni who so graciously lent me their time, advice, opinions, recollections, and stories: Executive producer and series creator Hugh Wilson; actors Howard Hesseman, Loni Anderson, Tim Reid, Richard Sanders, Gordon Jump, and Frank Bonner; and writers Blake Hunter, Tom Chehak, and Peter Torokvei. Each of these individuals provided me with a clearer picture and better understanding of *WKRP* in particular, and television in general. Furthermore, they have helped me realize that interesting television is the product of talented, dedicated, and caring individuals.

I particularly want to thank Blake Hunter, who has provided me with a number of valuable newspaper clippings and personal backstage photographs of the series. I would also like to give an extra-special thanks to Hugh Wilson, who has spoken with me a number of times in regard to the details and history of the show.

Chuck Schnable, who was the CBS-*WKRP* liaison during the first few seasons of the series, was also very helpful in providing a network point-of-view to this work.

Bart Andrews, author of a number of books on television, including *The I Love Lucy Book*, has also been a tremendous help.

Special thanks to Mickey Freeman, who helped me obtain an interview with Loni Anderson; Cynthia Snyder, who arranged for my interview with Frank Bonner; and Betty Ashley and Cynthia Webb of Warner Brothers, who helped me land a very fruitful interview with Howard Hesseman. I am also grateful to Gordon Jump's manager Curry Walls of Bauman-Hiller, and Richard Sanders' manager Steve Ross, from Abrams-Rubaloff & Lawrence. I would also like to thank Hugh Wilson's assistant, Deni, and Tim Reid's assistant, Brenda.

i

Extra-special thanks go to Jeff James of Nielsen Media Research in New York. Mr. James truly went above-and-beyond the call of duty in providing me with a great deal of ratings data regarding *WKRP*. I also want to express my warmest thanks to Lea A. Dantzler of *The Cincinnati Post*, who sent me a number of clippings regarding *WKRP*.

I must also thank all of the secretaries, office assistants, and other front-line people in countless offices in Los Angeles, New York, and Cincinnati who provided me with a great deal of help in obtaining information and interviews.

Closer to home, I am pleased to have the opportunity to thank University of Michigan-Flint professors Fred Svoboda and Bruce Rubenstein for their invaluable advice and support regarding both this project and my academic career. I also want to thank UM-Flint Professor Kenneth West for being there at the very beginning of this work. I am also very indebted to my publisher and editors, Pat Browne and Kathy Rogers Hoke of Popular Press, for their interest and support in this project.

Even closer to home, I want to thank my friends Hank Bryan, Mike Rose, and Marilyn Natchez for their friendship, loyalty, inspiration, and support. Also to my friend, Bob Hogan, who provided me with some great initial research.

Arriving as close to home as I can get, I want to express my love and thanks to my mother, my father, my brother Larry, my nieces Shiri and Michelle, my nephew Joshua, my sister-in-law Marilyn, and most of all, my wife Karen.

One last note: During our phone interview, Howard Hesseman told me that I need to stop watching *WKRP* re-runs and get out and enjoy life. I now pronounce myself ready to do just that.

WKRP Creative Alumni

Hugh Wilson: The very affable, personable, and talented Creator and Executive Producer of *WKRP in Cincinnati*.

Howard Hesseman: Played Johnny Fever, the personification of the rock-and-roll radio DJ. Wrote and directed for the series.

Loni Anderson: Brought life to the brainy and beautiful *WKRP* receptionist Jennifer Marlowe.

Gary Sandy: Portrayed the self-assured Program Director Andy Travis, who lead *WKRP* to top 40 success.

Tim Reid: Worked hard to present the human and emotional side of *WKRP* DJ Venus Flytrap. Wrote a number of poignant and important *WKRP* episodes.

Gordon Jump: Played the often-befuddled-yet-always-beloved Station Manger Arthur Carlson. Directed a *WKRP* episode.

Richard Sanders: Played the "funny hah-hah" newsman Les Nessman, whose hatred of communists and love of hogs provided the series with some of its funniest moments. Sanders also wrote a number of excellent episodes for the series.

Frank Bonner: Played the sleazy, kick-back taking, womanizing salesman Herb Tarlek. In addition to providing some surprisingly poignant moments to the series, Bonner also directed a number of *WKRP* episodes.

Chuck Schnable: CBS executive who, from 1978-1980, served as the liaison between the network and *WKRP*. Incredibly well liked by the rest of the *WKRP* alumni.

Blake Hunter: Writer and Producer for *WKRP*. The only original writer besides Hugh Wilson who was with the series all four seasons. Wrote some of *WKRP*'s most touching episodes. Became Executive Producer of *Who's the Boss?*

Tom Chehak: First season staff writer and producer. Went on to write for Fox Television's *Alien Nation*.

Peter Torokvei: Staff writer and producer who joined the series during its second season. Wrote some of *WKRP*'s most inventive episodes, including "Real Families."

Steven Kampmann: Staff writer and producer who joined the series during its second season. Also wrote a number of important episodes for the series.

Bill Dial: Original first season staff writer who wrote "Turkey's Away," *WKRP*'s most famous episode. Also appeared in a couple of episodes as *WKRP* engineer Bucky Dornster. Left the series after the first season. Became executive producer of the new first-run syndicated *WKRP* series.

Michael Fairman: Richard Sanders' *WKRP* writing partner who made a guest appearance as Buddy Baker in the *WKRP* episode "The Airplane Show."

Steve Marshall: Prolific *WKRP* Writer and producer.

Dan Guntzelman: Writer and Producer. Became Executive Producer of *Growing Pains*.

Sylvia Sidney: Played Momma Carlson in the pilot episode.

Carol Bruce: Replaced Sidney as Momma Carlson.

Allyn Ann McLerie: Played Carmen Carlson, Arthur's wife.

Edie McClurg: Played Lucille Tarlek, Herb's wife.

Max Tash: *WKRP* writer and producer. Tash and Wilson co-wrote one of *WKRP*'s best episodes, "Clean Up Radio Everywhere."

Lissa Levin: Wrote a number of important *WKRP* episodes.

Jay Sandrich: Veteran MTM director who directed the *WKRP* pilot.

Other Series Writers: Joyce Armor and Judy Neer, Casey Piotrowski, Paul Hunter, Jim Paddock, Mary Maguire, Gene Fournier and Tom Joachim, Bob Dolman, Jon Smet, Ben Elisco, and George Gaynes.

Other Series Directors: Michael Zinberg, Will MacKenzie, Rod Daniel, Asaad Kelada, Nicholas Stamos, Linda Day, Dolores Ferraro, George Gaynes.

Preface

I began working on this project over two years ago. Since that time, my ideas of the media and how I want to write about it have changed. I went into this project thinking that television is great, that the media is great, and that banal TV programming is only the result of a lack of talented writers. I still love television, but I no longer have very much faith in the media. A *Village Voice* writer once said that an episode of *WKRP* restored his faith in television; I feel that comment is misplaced, for the real hero is not the institution, but the small number of amazing individual actors, writers and producers who can rise above the economic restraints and illogical decisions of a media obsessed with maximum profits.

WKRP in Cincinnati is an example of a program crafted by amazing individuals who were able to transcend the confines of their medium. It is not so much a matter of *WKRP* being socially significant—although it was—for a TV show does not have to enlighten or take an stand in order for it to be of value. However, a TV show must entertain—and not in just some mindless manner. It must be well written, it must have interesting, three-dimensional characters, and, in the case of a sitcom, it must be funny. *WKRP* accomplished all of these goals; thus, it is a sitcom that demands study.

After reviewing the history of this show and talking with the caring and talented individuals involved in its production, I am convinced that quality television is a direct result of the talents' concern for details, accuracy, fairness, realism, and sincerity. While these concerns may not necessarily produce a hit, they will produce a quality program. More quality shows will ultimately lead to better television.

Therefore, rather than attack the media for its problems, I chose to celebrate the work of those who achieve quality in a medium that often tends to do everything possible to thwart such efforts. Hopefully, students of the media will take the words and wisdom of these talented individuals to heart. Ultimately, these students may then go on to create a new era of quality television. I can think of few actors and writers who set a better example for quality television than those who were involved in *WKRP*.

Introduction

There is something special about *WKRP in Cincinnati*. While it was never a sustained hit in prime-time, the hilarious, always "hip," often touching series does extremely well in syndication. It is *the* most popular MTM syndicated comedy, seen in more American markets than such MTM classics as *The Mary Tyler Moore Show* and *The Bob Newhart Show*. Although it never won an Emmy—it was nominated several times—the audience continues to award the show its loyalty. Furthermore, a new generation of fans are now finding, and falling in love with, *WKRP*.

This love affair with *WKRP* extends beyond our borders; the show plays in Japan, Mexico, Costa Rica, Italy, and dozens of other markets. "It's pretty widespread," says Howard Hesseman. "I mean on an international level. I got off a plane in Bangkok one day, from Singapore, and some little Thai Cat said to me, 'Crazy DJ!'—which I subsequently discovered is what the show is titled over there" (Hesseman).

Why do so many people tune in to the exploits of the "Crazy DJ" and his co-workers? What is it that makes *WKRP* so special? Before answering that question in detail, we can look at some of the brief explanations offered by several of *WKRP*'s stars and writers. Howard Hesseman feels that much of the show's success hinged on the dedication of those involved: "This isn't just some bullshit tip of the hat—these things don't happen, man, unless everybody is pitching in. And, that show was one in which a large percentage of the people really seemed to have a genuine commitment to doing the show—to making the show as good as it could possibly be, beyond what one normally encounters in 'the industry' " (Hesseman).

Gordon Jump agrees: "To every action, there's an equal and opposite reaction. It's a basic law of physics. And every one of those players that I played with—they never gave me back less than 100%" (Jump).

"Just about everybody who was there was very supportive," adds Richard Sanders. "Everybody did their work. There was nobody sluffing

1

off...There was no sort of thing like where you couldn't talk to another actor...you could always get them to help you out...It was a great thing. I had never had that experience before or since on any other show" (Sanders).

This dedication fostered an amazing attention to detail. Even the little things mattered. The control board in the studio, for instance, was laid out much like those found in real stations. All the knobs and buttons had specific functions, and the actors would virtually work the controls as they acted their part. Furthermore, actors and writers went to great lengths to maintain *WKRP*'s continuity. Blake Hunter, one of the show's original writers, kept a journal listing the various "facts" mentioned in each episode, rendering the sitcom more consistent—and the station more realistic. A station general manager once told Gordon Jump, "You know, I used to laugh at your show until I realized I'm watching a documentary."

Hugh Wilson, creator, executive producer and head writer of the series, was frequently complimented on the show's realism. "I got so many letters like that," said Wilson. "...So many people who worked for radio stations literally wrote in and said, 'You must have researched at the station I work at.' I know for a fact that we certainly captured the spirit of the thing...and I was very proud of that...We tried to behave ourselves on *WKRP*...I think the truth is much more interesting than fiction" (Wilson).

More important than providing a realistic setting, however, was *WKRP*'s attention to character development. *WKRP* Staff writer Tom Chehak said, "I think the characters were really thoroughly defined. The thing with a half-hour [sitcom is that]...if people understand the characters, understand where they're coming from, you've got 'em...Well, that's what happened in *WKRP*—You knew if Herb Tarlek walked into the room, or [Jennifer] walked into the room, between Frank and Loni, there was a laugh,—or a look from the Big Guy—whatever. And they were so clearly defined and so clearly different, you could write any situation; they had all kinds of attitudes" (Chehak).

"It was real," added Gordon Jump. "It was believable. It was about fallible people. We saw the good and the bad in all of us, and, I think, in the humor and in the writing, it was a very honest presentation that everybody could identify with—I think that's what makes a successful television show" (Jump).

Hugh Wilson was well aware of the importance of having three-dimensional characters. To Wilson, the story and the integrity of the characters were more important than even the jokes. Said Hesseman: "I—all my life—will be indebted to Hugh Wilson for...consistently saying the bottom line is that, no matter how funny the joke is, if it gets in the way of the story it has to go. He was a guy who really wanted the stories to be clear and for the characters to come through...To me, that's as close to good as it gets in sitcoms."

This attention to character development is rare among sitcom producers. "...I'm always amazed at how a lot of successful TV shows can remain so superficial after being on the air...," said Wilson. "I mean 90 [episodes of *WKRP*]—that's 45 hours. And a lot of shows, *Laverne and Shirley* [for instance]—they've got 300 [episodes]. It's 150 hours later and you don't really know much more about them than you did in the beginning. Maybe that's unfair because I didn't watch that show...but I have a suspicion it's probably true" (Wilson).

For all the attention to character and realism, humor was the main appeal of *WKRP*. It was also a very "hip" show in that not all of the jokes were aimed at the average viewer. "You know what?" commented Wilson. "They'd come up with a joke and say that it would never play in Peoria. And they'd throw it out. My theory was, 'To hell with it—let's put it in there...they'll just think it's a straight line...I got a funny joke coming up here that everybody will understand, but let's do this for the people who would appreciate it...Why take it out? What if only 10 percent get it? Why is that bad?' " (Wilson).

While *WKRP* presented a number of issue-oriented shows, it never preached its message. In an era of sitcoms that attack relevant issues with the same light touch of a robotic jazz band, *WKRP* provided a refreshing change. "Maybe [it's] because of Hugh's influence and the fact that he was always much more interested in people than in any particular issue," said series writer Peter Torokvei. "And, of course, that's where comedy comes from—it's what drama is all about. And that's what we always concentrated on; where these characters—where these people—were in their thinkings and feelings and thoughts" (Torokvei).

"I think that Hugh Wilson has got to be 99 percent of the reason for the success of the show," added Tim Reid. The rest of the *WKRP* alumni agree (Reid).

4 America's Favorite Radio Station

So, why has *WKRP* gone critically unacclaimed for so long? "Well, you know, maybe it's like great literature," suggested Torokvei. "I've always believed that great literature, in its own time, was never recognized. That it isn't until later that people start to see that it's a better show" (Torokvei).

Following is a look at the history and significance of *WKRP*, a show that Hesseman described as, "some of the best radio on television." Most likely, Hesseman is right, but it goes much deeper than that; *WKRP in Cincinnati* was some of the best television on television, as well.

Chapter One
The Concept

Harrison's is a bar in Atlanta that caters to the advertising and media crowd. It was there, in the early 1970s, Hugh Wilson met radio WQXI salesman Clark Brown. Through Brown, along with others in the media, Wilson had the chance to meet a number of the people who worked in Atlanta radio. Although he did not realize it at the time, these friendships proved valuable to Wilson's creation of *WKRP in Cincinnati*.

Hugh Wilson's affable manner and light drawl reveal his Southeastern, Coral Gables, Florida upbringing. A humble person, he was blessed with both a sense of humor and a sense of values. In talking with those who have worked with him, it is impossible to find anything but praise for Wilson's ability and demeanor. He is the type who will fight for what he believes in and make compromises only when doing so will promise a better end result. Furthermore, rather than use his power as a producer to simply promote himself, Wilson has helped start or advance the careers of countless other writers and producers. In an age where everyone looks for specialists, Wilson realizes that track records are secondary to a good sense of humor and creative potential.

Part of Wilson's commitment to developing new talent may stem from his own rise to fame. Having worked his way up from a number of less-than-glamorous positions—he was once an office copier salesman with an "all-residential" territory (Graham)—Wilson is living proof of the American Dream. After graduating from college, he took a job with the Armstrong Cork Company, where he wrote about luminaire ceilings for an architectural trade magazine. At Armstrong, Wilson met fellow writers Jay Tarses and Tom Patchett, who, after working as stand-up comics, eventually went to Hollywood and began writing for and producing *The Bob Newhart Show*. Meanwhile, Wilson moved to Atlanta to pursue a career in advertising.

Wilson, who made several attempts at film making while in Atlanta, maintained his friendship with Jay and Tom. In 1975 the two set up an

5

interview between Wilson and Grant Tinker, then head of MTM Enterprises. Impressed with what he saw, Tinker hired Wilson as a writer for *The Bob Newhart Show*. From there, Wilson, Patchett, Tarses and Gary David Goldberg wrote for *The Tony Randall Show*. Randall, who played Philadelphia Court of Common Pleas Judge Walter Franklin, took a liking to Wilson, who eventually became one of the show's producers.

In 1977, Tinker asked Wilson and Goldberg to submit pilot ideas for the upcoming fall season. Goldberg came up with a series that featured the antics of a Black World War II flying squadron. Wilson began "noodling" and soon approached Tinker with an idea for a "character comedy" concerning a radio station. "Ideas in themselves are never interesting to me," recalled Tinker in a 1978 interview. "It's always a matter of execution. What was interesting is that Hugh is a good writer and has enthusiasm." A week later, Tinker and Wilson met with Andrew Siegel, vice president for comedy development at CBS. Siegel was impressed and gave Wilson the go-ahead to write a pilot script (Graham).

Before developing the characters for his series, Wilson returned to Atlanta and called upon his old friend Clark Brown. Spending the day at WQXI, a successful AM/FM rocker, Wilson began to people the staff of his fictional station. Brown, who dressed in traditional salesman fashion, found himself on Wilson's growing list of characters as none other than Herbert R. Tarlek, Executive Sales Manager of WKRP AM radio.

While WQXI was the model for WKRP, television's limitations forced Wilson to make some changes. "Most of these stations have a sales force," recalled Wilson. " 'Quixy' had six salesmen. I figured that might be out. We would only have one salesman, which led me to the course that I probably would have taken anyhow—WKRP would not be a real successful station" (Wilson).

This realized, Wilson arrived at the basic format of the show. WKRP had been a radio station that was stumbling around at the bottom end of the ratings. In an attempt at success, the station manager hires a new program director to turn the station around. Part of the new program director's plans include changing the station's "elevator music" format to rock and roll. The character who would make those changes was Andy Travis.

Wilson based Travis on his cousin, whose name, interestingly enough, is Andy Travis. Although the real Travis is a policeman in

Colorado, Wilson borrowed elements from his cousin's personality—his fondness for cowboy hats, for example—in developing the fictional Travis personality.

With the format change idea in place, Wilson created his DJs. While WKRP would be a 24-hour radio station, Wilson realized that there would have to be several DJs who were never seen on camera. Wilson's prototype for one of the featured DJs, Johnny Fever, was WQXI's Skinny Bobby Harper. "Skinny Bobby was one of those guys who was never quite awake because he had to get up at four in the morning to get in there," said Wilson. "I would see him and he would say, 'God damn, I worked at twenty stations in the last ten years,' you know, that type of thing. A little bit of burnout and also alimony. Kind of past it. Now he's a very successful DJ in Atlanta at WSB" (Wilson).

The other DJ Wilson created was Venus Flytrap, a wild dressing black man who had come up from New Orleans to join the WKRP staff. Admittedly used as a vehicle to "scare the hell out of WKRP station owner Momma Carlson," Wilson would leave it until later to decide upon Flytrap's real name and character.

Wilson also realized he would need a news director, leading him to Les Nessman. Not based on any particular person he had known, Wilson described Nessman as an "anal-retentive, string collector." Wilson had great empathy for the character. "He's in such an ugly position to be the news guy at a rock station. You know how much attention they pay to news. A man that deeply admired Ed Murrow and all the great broadcast journalists of history—to have that poor fellow stuck in a station where they did five minutes of news on the hour!" (Wilson).

Wilson rounded out his cast with Arthur C. Carlson, the station manager; Bailey Quarters, who did the station's commercial scheduling; and Jennifer Marlowe, the knock-out blonde receptionist.

Wilson says that Arthur Carlson was not based on anyone at WQXI, but he admits that he had known someone like Carlson. "We had a line on the show once—'When the going gets tough, the tough get going.' And, to Carlson, that meant getting your hat and getting the shit out of there" (Wilson).

According to Gordon Jump, who played Carlson, part of the character was based on an actual WQXI radio executive, whose many Carlson-like antics have become legend in radio history. "[This man] is an institution in American Broadcasting," said Jump. "He was not only the man who did the turkey drop for a station...in Dallas, Texas (which was later reprised in one of *WKRP*'s most famous episodes, "Turkey's Away"), but he also did another promotion in Atlanta that got him in trouble with the Society for the Prevention of Cruelty to Animals. He put ducks in the window of a downtown department store and invited everybody to come down and see the 'Quixy Quacker Dancing Ducks.' And the ducks really did dance, but, in effect what was done was a hotplate was apparently placed under [the ducks]. And they were moving their little tootsies to keep from burning" (Jump).

Bailey Quarters, the shy yet ambitious commercial scheduler at WKRP, was based on Wilson's wife. Bailey was to represent the women in the work force who wanted desperately to be considered professionals, yet were not "ballsy" or pushy enough to be taken seriously (Wilson).

Wilson then created *WKRP*'s most controversial character, the beautiful-yet-wise Jennifer Marlowe. To Wilson's knowledge, Jennifer had no real-world counterpart; Wilson claims he had never run across a receptionist as beautiful as Jennifer. Much has been written about the possible "jiggle" factor Jennifer was to lend the show—remember, *Charlie's Angels* had made its debut just two years earlier. The critics' pans aside, however, Jennifer was no mere ratings device.

His "staff" assembled, Wilson went back to Hollywood to write the script. "What I wanted to do," recalled Wilson, "was inject a thread of madness and insanity into television" (Fong-Torres). Throwing out draft after draft, Wilson came up with the final version sometime around the 1977 Christmas weekend. CBS paid Wilson $25,000 for the pilot script (Graham).

TV Before WKRP

It is important to understand some of the changes in the television climate that had taken place before the debut of *WKRP*. Many critics will agree that, in the early 1970s, television began to more accurately reflect its times. This was due, in large part, to the contributions made by Mary Tyler Moore Enterprises and Norman Lear and Bud Yorkin's Tandem Productions. Before the appearance of shows like *The Mary Tyler Moore Show* and *All in the Family*, standard TV sitcom fare consisted of wacky shows like *My Mother the Car* or rural comedies such as *The Andy Griffith Show*, *The Beverly Hillbillies* and *Green*

Acres. While it is common critical tradition to pan such shows as *The Beverly Hillbillies* or *Green Acres*, these sitcoms were not only amusing but also well written and very popular. *The Beverly Hillbillies*, an overnight success, dominated the ratings for the duration of its run (Cox). What was it, then, that shifted the viewer's attention from rural rollicking to metropolitan involvement?

It all has to do with ratings, or, rather, how the ratings were being interpreted. Before 1970, ratings were based on the raw, total number of people watching a particular show. In the late-1960s and early-1970s, networks began to evaluate shows by using demographics. The argument was that, while a show may attract more people, those viewers may not represent the upscale market that advertisers wanted to reach. Ratings were broken into age, gender and social groupings so that advertisers could learn what sort of people were watching what sort of shows.[1]

In order to reach the more upscale, purchase-oriented group, the networks decided to air more sophisticated shows. This action was spearheaded by Bob Wood, who became president of CBS in 1970. Someone once remarked, "When Bob Wood became president of CBS, he canceled every show with a tree in it" (Winship 65).

Though the networks made attempts with shows such as *Julia* and *Room 222* in the late 1960s, the first really ground-breaking sitcom was *All in the Family*. Although ABC had first crack at the Tandem production, they passed it up to let CBS chart the new waters (McCrohan 18). CBS, which, at the time, was the leader in television comedy, could afford to take chances with a show such as *All in the Family*. In the end, that strategy paid off.

One year earlier, MTM Enterprises, headed by Mary Tyler Moore and her then-husband Grant Tinker, approached sophistication via a different route. In the 1960s, Mary Tyler Moore had become a television favorite from her days playing Laura Petrie on *The Dick Van Dyke Show*. After a failed attempt at a movie career, Moore and Tinker set up MTM productions to produce a show for CBS. Unlike the loud, often obnoxious image of *All in the Family*, MTM had a more urbane format.

Though never approaching the success of *All in the Family* (Brooks, Marsh 808-10). *The Mary Tyler Moore Show* was unique because it was the first sitcom to present a woman who was 30 and single by choice (in the original version of the show Mary Richards was a divorcee, but apparently even CBS was not ready for that). The sitcom also brought into vogue the ensemble cast, in which each of the characters—not one or two main characters—served to fuel both the humor and the situation. So successful was this approach that other production companies began to adopt the format.

Not only did Mary Tyler Moore receive critical and popular acclaim for her show, but she and Grant Tinker were able to turn MTM Enterprises into a highly respected production company that became known for its quality programming.[2] MTM shows stressed writing and the idea of character development over pure, raw laughs. While the MTM shows attacked contemporary concerns, their approach was more subtle than Tandem's *All in the Family, Maude* or *Good Times*. This led to a very polished, sophisticated style that was repeated with great success in such shows as *Rhoda* and *The Bob Newhart Show*, as well as in highly regarded sitcoms like *Paul Sand in Friends and Lovers*, and *The Tony Randall Show*. While the MTM shows were each unique, they all shared a common quality feel. Much as with a brand-name product, viewers could tell the difference between an MTM show and a Tandem show.

As if someone had said "enough of reality," or "enough of this quality stuff," in the mid to late-1970 shows such as *Happy Days*, *Laverne and Shirley*, and *Mork and Mindy* began to dominate TV schedules. With wonderman Fred Silverman at the helm of ABC, which toppled the other networks in the late 1970s, CBS and NBC struggled to produce their own brand of mindless pap. Even the Lear Shows began to take a wicked turn, with programs such as *Different Strokes* and, later, *The Facts of Life*. However, MTM was able to maintain its level of quality programming, not only in comedy, but in drama as well, with shows like *Lou Grant*, and, later, *The White Shadow, Hill Street Blues*. and *St. Elsewhere*. Flying in the face of the "great uglying of American sitcoms," MTM continued their commitment to quality with *WKRP in Cincinnati*.

"There's Money on the Ground out Here..."

According to a 1978 *Wall Street Journal* article, the concept of *WKRP* was fortuitous. "Three seasons back ABC had toppled CBS from its long standing preeminence in the Nielsen ratings with a strategy of scheduling comedies aimed at young audiences in the early evening hours, when the kids control the nation's sets," wrote Ellen Graham.

"Now CBS was avidly searching for the same sort of comedy to rebuild its early evening line-up. 'The guts of any evening is the nine to 10 time period...,' says Donald B. Grant, CBS's programming vice president. 'If you have strong lead-ins in the early evening, you win the night' " (Graham).

Despite *WKRP*'s promise to deliver the best of both worlds—a young audience and quality production—as the 1978 series development season drew to a close, Tinker couldn't get CBS to commit to producing the pilot. "I told [CBS] I'd been reading about other projects CBS had chosen, and I said I thought it was odd they hadn't given us a go," recalled Tinker to Graham. According to Tinker, CBS, in an almost off-handed response to Tinker's complaint, agreed to allow MTM to make the pilot. The network agreed to pick up most of the pilot's $300,000 production tab (Graham).

After Wilson was made the show's producer, he quickly began assembling his writing/production staff. According to Graham, Wilson called his old friend Bill Dial, an Atlanta newspaperman, and said, "There's money on the ground out here, come on out." Wilson also hired friends Blake Hunter, a Los Angeles copy writer, and Tom Chehak, a production assistant that Wilson had met while they were both working on *The Bob Newhart Show*. To Wilson, hiring people with little or no background in TV sitcom writing was an advantage. "I wanted people who didn't know all the old jokes and tricks," he told Graham. Wilson was also happy to be working with friends. "In script sessions, you have to feel you're in a safe place so you can pitch the gawd-awfulest jokes without making a fool of yourself," noted Wilson. "If you start editing in your head, it kills the spontaneity" (Graham).

Armed with an excellent script, a commitment from CBS, and a friendly camp of writers, Wilson strode toward the next hurdle: casting *WKRP*.

Chapter Two
Casting *WKRP*
"The Worst Three Weeks of My Life"

You have just been transported to the late 1970s, where you are casting a new television show. Perhaps you've dreamed of the opportunity to play the glamorous Hollywood casting director; however, there is more than the glitter and glitz to consider. Not only do your choices influence the success of a $300,000 pilot, but the possible ad revenues—millions of dollars—should your series become a hit. You're not just gambling with your own career, but with the careers of many actors, writers, and producers as well. If your pilot makes it to the fall schedule, $2 million of network money will be tied up in the first thirteen episodes. The success or failure of your show will also have an effect on other shows in the surrounding line-up. Suddenly the glamour turns into pressure—the exact pressure felt by Hugh Wilson and casting director Bob Manahan as they set out to find the perfect cast for *WKRP in Cincinnati*. It is no wonder that Wilson recalled the period as the "worst three weeks in my life" (Graham).

While the success of a sitcom hinges on many factors, casting is key. Of what value is a great script or a great director without a great cast to bring the work to life? Good casting is not simply a search for talented actors; it is a quest to uncover people who will work well together.

As an MTM show, casting was crucial; *WKRP* had a legacy of legendary casts with which to compete. Much of the magic of MTM classics such as *The Mary Tyler Moore Show* or *The Bob Newhart Show* was derived from the balletic interplay of the shows' actors. For example, it was not just Mary Richards interacting with Lou Grant, but Mary Tyler Moore as Mary Richards interacting with Ed Asner as Lou Grant. The contributions of both these stars transcended anything that could have been accomplished through writing or directing. That is the magic of casting—the magic Wilson was after.

There are a number of qualities casting directors want. In 1978, Arnold Becker, vice president of national research at CBS around the time of *WKRP*'s debut, told *Wall Street Journal* writer Ellen Graham that "Love is a very important [sitcom] ingredient." Also important is finding a cast that can function as a family (Graham). *WKRP* was in good hands with Manahan, who had cast the lovable family ensembles of *The Bob Newhart Show* and *The Tony Randall Show*. However, no matter how skilled or experienced the casting team is, ingredients such as love and family are never guaranteed. Thus, a great deal of *WKRP*'s magic hinged on luck. According to Frank Bonner, who played Herb Tarlek, casting is a crap shoot: "*WKRP* was a magic mix of characters that worked. Had it been another blonde, had it been another Herb, had it been another Johnny Fever, it may not have worked out as well. They just get actors together and they hope that they work together. It's kind of a melting pot that you throw [all of the actors] into and stir it up into a nice, wonderful stew and hope it comes out" (Bonner).

Wilson began to prepare his "stew." With only three weeks to complete this formidable task, Wilson, casting director Bob Manahan, Mary Tyler Moore, Grant Tinker, and other casting executives from CBS set out to find an appealing, lovable family that America would welcome into its homes. "You let these people into your living rooms," said Becker to Graham. "They have to be nice folks or [people] don't want them" (Graham).

"It Was the Part of His Life"
Howard Hesseman

It was fate—perhaps destiny—that Howard Hesseman came to play Johnny Fever. Aside from Hesseman's weather-worn, disheveled features being well suited to the role—he looked like a man who had been "packing and unpacking up and down the dial"—consider the chance meetings that had been taking place between him and Wilson:

Howard and Hugh first met in Atlanta in 1974, when Hesseman was touring with *The Committee*, a highly respected improvisational comedy group. An avid fan of the group, Wilson, who was still in advertising at the time, went backstage to talk with Hesseman and the company. One year later, Wilson and Hesseman ran into each other on the set of *The Bob Newhart Show*, where Hesseman was playing Craig Plager, one of Dr. Robert Hartley's patients. The next year, Hesseman and Wilson met again, this time on the set of *The Tony Randall Show*.

None of these meetings, however, sparked any true bond of friendship—the two were just acquaintances who had no idea of the profound impact their talent would have on each others lives. "We didn't realize we were about to meet again until I got in the room with him," said Hesseman, recalling his 1978 *WKRP* audition with Wilson. "And he's saying, 'Oh, it's you...' And I'm saying, 'Yeah, you're the guy—oh, okay' "(Hesseman).

Hesseman, an only child who suffered from asthma, was born in 1940 in Salem, Oregon. His early life was not easy. Hesseman's parents were divorced when he was five. His mother later remarried, and Hesseman became very close to his stepfather. Hesseman knew very little of his real father, who died in 1954 (Hoover, Riley 113).

After graduating from high school in 1958, Hesseman spent the summer in San Francisco before returning to the University of Oregon to study theater. It was there that he met his first wife; the marriage only lasted six months. Two years later, Hesseman married a jeweler from San Francisco. That marriage lasted a bit longer—four years (Hano 23). The two ex-wives gave Hesseman a closer connection to Dr. Johnny Fever, who was also twice divorced.

Though he never completed his work at the university, Hesseman, going by the name of Don Sturdy, began working as an actor. In 1965, he obtained his first of many episodic roles. "Gary Marshall gave a lot of us early TV work," recalled Hesseman. "That was through somebody who was a casting director at the time over at Paramount—Fred Rouse...He put me in my first two *Andy Griffith* shows. I think in the first episode I was working at a carnival. I think my line was, 'Mustard on that?' Something like that—that kind of stuff" (Hesseman).

Eventually, the parts got better. Hesseman is particularly proud of his work with *The Committee*. Starting with the group in 1965, Hesseman worked six days a week doing political satire and comedy. *The Committee* launched many other careers, as well, including actors Rob Reiner and Penny Marshall. Furthermore, many former *Committee* people later found character roles on *WKRP* (Hesseman).

In 1967, Hesseman worked part-time as a DJ at KMPX in San Francisco. Part of the pioneering underground radio movement, Hesseman played a mix of rock, acid-rock, and folk. "What's always been bollixed in every interview is the fact that I was working full time as an actor and had been doing so for over two years as a member of *The Committee*....before I did this stint as a favor to the late Tom Donahue on KMPX," said Hesseman. "It isn't as though I worked in radio and then became an actor. I'd been doing plays on a non-professional basis for a number of years, and had been working professionally for two, two-and-one-half years before I did this six hours every Saturday radio shot for about eight or nine months [Radio] was never a serious career choice" (Hesseman).

Indeed, before *WKRP*, Hesseman guested on a number of shows, including *Dragnet*, *The Hottest Place in Town*, *Rhoda*, *The Blue Knight*, *Switch*, *Mary Hartman, Mary Hartman*, and *Laverne & Shirley*. He has been in the theatrical releases *Billy Jack* and *Silent Movie*, and appeared in the TV movies *Howard: The Amazing Mr. Hughes* and *The Ghost of Flight 401* (Parish, Terrance 151).

Hesseman was working on *Soap* when he heard about *WKRP*. Jay Sandrich, a seasoned director who had done a great deal of work on *The Mary Tyler Moore Show*, was directing *Soap* at the time. Having been selected by MTM to direct the *WKRP* pilot, Sandrich suggested that Hesseman audition for Hugh Wilson. In the meantime, Sandrich told Wilson to take a look at Hesseman—Jay was sure that Hesseman had a lot to offer the series.

During a lunch break from *Soap*, Hesseman left the ABC studios and drove over to the valley to MTM/CBS. Waiting in Wilson's outer office, Hesseman was given some scenes that Wilson and staff writer Bill Dial had wanted him to read. "[I] asked the secretary if there was a full script I could look at," continues Hesseman. "I just read it quickly—like a 40 or 50 page script—just sort of skimmed it to get the general structure of the story.

"I had the sense, then, walking into the inner office...that, yeah, this DJ character was really interesting—that Jay Sandrich was right. That I could do this guy and offer some excitement" (Hesseman).

However, there was a problem: Wilson was interested in having Hesseman read for the part of Herb Tarlek not Johnny Fever. Frank Bonner, who ended up getting the Tarlek role, finds this incredible: "Howard *is* Johnny Fever!" (Bonner).

Hesseman agreed to read for the part, but he was only humoring Wilson and Dial: "It was clear to me then, on the basis of a quick reading of the script in an outer office, and [in] talking with them, that I was only interested in the role of Johnny Caravella. The character seemed rife with possibilities, and in talking with Hugh and Bill Dial...I sensed that things I was saying were meeting with their approval....If I had something to say about the character, they seemed to agree and be able to add that to the vision they already had. So, we were a little further toward, at least, on the level of a preliminary discussion—co-creating the character.

"...I was just letting them know that I had—off the top of my head —a lot of ideas about the guy. And the feedback that I was getting was that they liked my ideas...That was based on a brief encounter with the script" (Hesseman).

Realizing that DJs are the most identifiable human portion of radio, Hesseman's desire to do the part grew stronger. "That was the flash for me in reading the script initially and on starting to work on it in the production period," said Hesseman. "...This was an opportunity to give life to a character that exists in semi-mythic proportions in virtually everybody's mind under 40 years-of-age in America.

"...There is one specific jock who exists in people's minds—you hear the voice. It's like you hear that one specific song that always makes you think of incredible incidents that occurred when you were listening to that song. I can remember jocks from when I was growing up in Oregon. But, you don't really know what they look like when they're doing their job...So the disk jockey, like I said in one show, 'just sort of lives in the airwaves for the people.' He really is a kind of semi-invisible person who exists with and in and of all this music that he's playing. Well, I thought it was a great opportunity to create a character that everybody sort of thinks of themselves as knowing, without really knowing much about that character" (Hesseman).

Impressed as they were with Hesseman, Wilson and Dial had already committed themselves to another actor. According to first-season staff writer Tom Chehak, Wilson had awarded the Fever role to actor Dick Libertini, who, among other things, had worked in *The Melba Moore—Clifton Davis Show*, and had played The Godfather in *Soap*. When Libertini opted to do a *Movie of the Week* instead of the *WKRP* pilot, Hesseman won the role (Chehak).

"Hesseman—," sighs Wilson. "If there ever was a part written for someone—Hesseman dressed like Fever dressed, and Hesseman was kind of anti-social—the gad fly—it was the part of his life" (Wilson).

"I Looked Like the Guy that Did the Turkey Drop."
Gordon Jump

It was not difficult for Gordon Jump to relate to the life of a Cincinnati broadcaster. Since his college graduation, Jump had worked in a number of local radio and television stations. What's more, he was born and raised in Centerville, Ohio, which lies halfway between Dayton and Cincinnati. In scenes where Arthur Carlson would speak fondly of Ohio, Jump was speaking from his heart. "Cincinnati was a favorite town of mine," reflected Jump.

Upon graduating from Centerville High, Jump attended Ohio's Otterbine College. After his freshman year, Jump studied broadcasting and communications at Kansas State University in Topeka. Degree in hand, he landed a job in a Topeka radio station. From there, Jump went on to various local radio and television stations. "I did some announcing. I did writing, producing and directing...In small stations like that in the beginning years of television, you did everything."

"Everything" included a stint as "WIB the Clown" on WIBW in Topeka. "I...hosted cartoons and created my own little educational vignettes," said Jump. "We'd take little things that would be graphic demonstrations of some physical phenomenon—putting an egg at the top of a milk bottle at bedtime and heating it up, so, when the bottle would cool down, the egg went 'plop' into the bottle. Talking about the changing air pressure—stuff of that nature. But, we did it with fun."

Playing "WIB" was not Jump's only on-air function at WIBW. "I would turn around and do the weather," recalled Jump. "It was a little embarrassing at times because sometimes I didn't quite get the make-up off as well as I might have. You could see this faint image of a rather broad clown mouth on my face as I was trying to do the weather. I would try to face the board more than the camera so that we could cover that up."

In 1963, while Jump was working in, of all things, Ohio radio, he decided to venture to California and try his hand at acting. It was a gutsy move for the 32-year-old who had already established himself in the broadcasting industry. Diving into the bigger pond meant giving up the security of the local markets. After working bit parts for five to seven years, the career started paying off.

Jump got his first episodic guest appearance through CBS

Producer/Director Paul King. Jump played Samuel Clemens in an episode of *Daniel Boone*. From there, Jump landed a number of character parts on programs such as *Green Acres*, *The Partridge Family*, *The New Dick Van Dyke Show*, *Good Times*, and *The Black Sheep Squadron*. For MTM, Jump worked in *The Mary Tyler Moore Show* and *Paul Sand in Friends and Lovers*. He also appeared with fellow *WKRP* actor Richard Sanders in the TV movie *Ruby and Oswald*.

In 1977, Jump captured a recurring role on *Soap*. Although Hesseman was also working in the series that same year, Jump recalls that "the show was so busy, we never had a chance to really develop a friendship." As had happened with Hesseman, director Jay Sandrich proved instrumental in getting Jump a meeting with Wilson.

Jump first got wind of the *WKRP* pilot from actor Eugene Roche, whose episodic work included playing Frank Flynn in the short-lived 1973 ABC comedy *The Corner Bar*. Roche had recently auditioned for the Carlson character. "I think they're interested in me, but I'm not sure that they want to pay my kind of money," Roche told Jump.

This piqued Jump's curiosity. "I kept thinking at the time," said Jump, " 'Gee, it would be wonderful to create a character...from the very beginning of a show.'

"Eugene had been around a lot longer than I had, but, apparently, as good an actor as Eugene was, he wasn't physically what they were looking for. Jay Sandrich...told Hugh Wilson...'Why don't you take a look at Gordon Jump? I don't know if he's what you're looking for, but if he is, he can certainly read the lines'."

Five days before the pilot rehearsals began, Wilson took Sandrich's advice and sent for Jump. "Thursday afternoon he brought me in and looked at me and he just guffawed—he laughed out loud," remembered Jump. "I thought, 'Gee, I must be doing a wonderful job.' The truth was that I looked like the [radio executive] who did the turkey drop, who happened to be a gentleman who [then] managed a station in Atlanta, Georgia, called 'Quixy' [WQXI]."

Jump's resemblance to the radio executive was not just a stroke of luck for him, but for Wilson, as well. Indeed, part of the magic of casting involves the proper selection of types. "The look is [very] important, as far as Hollywood producers and casting directors are concerned," commented Jump. "...They want what they see, because what they see will be consistent. They don't want it to be acted or contrived.

"Hugh [basically] hired me on the spot. By the time I was home, my agent was calling me saying, 'You have a job.'

"...It was a wonderful opportunity. I was able to bring my chemistry to the group, which [included] my understanding of the industry and my understanding of people that run local television and local radio stations. I'd worked with them. I knew them. I had characters to draw from."

Once Jump was cast, Wilson asked him to read with several hopefuls competing for the Andy Travis role. The day after snaring the part—a Friday—Jump went to CBS and screen tested with seven actors. "After I finished the screen test, I came home and I said to my wife, 'You know, one actor and I really had great chemistry; It's going to be interesting to see who Grant and Mary Tyler Moore and Jay Sandrich pick—as well as Hugh Wilson.' And, when I went in Monday...the person that they had picked was the one that I felt I had great chemistry with. That was Gary Sandy" (Jump).

"The Main Driver of the Car"
Gary Sandy

Though Wilson found that some of the actors "only had to say six words and we knew we had our character," casting for other roles was more difficult (Graham). Such was the case with the Andy Travis character, which was not cast until two days before rehearsals for the pilot began. Spending the weekend watching test tapes, Wilson, Mary Tyler Moore, Grant Tinker, and other CBS casting executives narrowed down the field of seven hopefuls. The task was not without its own complications; "We all picked a different guy," said Grant Tinker (Graham).

The problem was finding a straight character who could interact with the rest of the "zanies" that populated *WKRP*. "In order to carry the ball," said Wilson to Graham, "the main driver of the car has to be likable and sane, with all of the nuts hanging off of the fender."

If Austin Sandy would have had his way, his son Gary would have been a sportscaster, a profession the elder Sandy considered to be very prestigious. Had it not been for a twist of fate, Gary's father may have gotten his wish.

Sandy, also an Ohio native, was reared in Kettering, a suburb of Dayton, where Sandy's father worked as a safety engineer for the

Frigidaire corporation. As a student at Fairmont High, Sandy became involved with the debate team. In 1964, Sandy worked his way through regional competition to the semi-finals held at Ohio State University. However, a technicality kept him out of the competition.

Winning the championship would have meant a college scholarship. Sandy was heartbroken. Austin was equally upset; his dreams of Gary being a sportscaster were seemingly dashed. When his speech teacher made a last minute switch and entered Sandy in the one-act play competition, however, Sandy took home a championship in drama and was named All-State actor. Sandy enrolled in Wilmington College to study theater under Hugh Heiland. For three years, Sandy studied all aspects of theater and appeared in some 30 college productions. Impressed by Sandy's talent, Heiland advised the young actor to go to New York. Sandy was flattered by his mentor's suggestion, but, not wanting to disappoint his father, decided to enroll in an Atlanta broadcasting school. The experience proved that Sandy's heart was not in broadcasting. Leaving the program behind, he went to New York to further his acting studies at the Academy of Dramatic Arts.

Sandy helped to pay his tuition and living expenses by working as a Broadway ticket agent. Though he got a lot of tickets to some great shows, Sandy had trouble attaining his own ticket to fame—or, at least, to gainful employment as an actor. After graduating from the Academy, Sandy went a year without a single part—he could not even find work in commercials. Then, he got the chance to read for the role of a returning, disillusioned Vietnam vet on *As the World Turns*. "I'll never understand casting directors," recalled Sandy in an interview in *TV Guide*. "They said I was too wholesome and bubbly for a Vietnam vet, but I'd be great as the malicious college roommate who hooks him on dope" (Davidson 24).

Over the next five and one-half years, Sandy played a number of soap characters that *TV Guide* described as "deceptively-wholesome looking villains." After his stint as the drug-pushing roommate on *As the World Turns*, Sandy played a rough-with-the-ladies river-boat casino manager on *Somerset*. As Stace Reddin in *The Secret Storm*, Sandy's character tried to rape the illicit fiance of his brother, a Catholic priest. These types of roles extended into Sandy's prime time work, as well. On *Starsky and Hutch*, Sandy played a "psychopathic killer who squashed his victims with a sawed-off baseball bat by night and spent his days curled up in a catatonic stupor." Even in film, Sandy was cast in a less-than-flattering light—he played a "demented" truck driver in the movie *The Great Smokey Road Block* (Davidson 24).

Working as a regular in Norman Lear's syndicated comedy *All that Glitters*, Sandy caught the attention of CBS casting executive Mike Olton. Impressed by what he saw, Olton suggested Sandy to Wilson. With parts that painted Sandy as more of a "nut hanging off of the fender" than "the main driver of the car," Olton decided not to tell Wilson about Sandy's previous roles.

"I never watched *All that Glitters*," reflected Wilson in a *TV Guide* interview, "and I don't watch daytime TV. All I knew was that we had tested a lot of people for the part and here, suddenly, was a nice-looking All American Boy-type guy who knew how to act and had a keen comedic sense. He looked good in a cowboy hat...And he reacted marvelously in the test with Gordon Jump... (Davidson 26).

"We watched Gary's film test, along with several other tests, on a Saturday. Mary Tyler Moore was the first to say, 'It's no contest. Gary Sandy's the fellow we've been looking for.' We all agreed and two days later...we started filming the pilot" (Davidson 26).

"Miss Everything"
Loni Anderson

It should come as no surprise that Loni Anderson had won a number of beauty contests. Inspired by her mother, who worked as a runway fashion model, Anderson had been competing in beauty contests since she was a little girl. "I was Queen of the First Grade, Queen of the Second Grade—if there was a contest or a play, I was in it," recalled Anderson. An independent girl, in order to save money for college she worked at a number of jobs and modeled for many of the local stores in her home town of Minneapolis. Anderson won such titles as "Miss Thermo-Jac Clothing," "Miss Country Style Ford," "Miss Tom McAn Shoes," "Miss No-Frost Eskimo," and "Queen of the Hole-In-One." "I was Miss Everything," noted Anderson (Torgerson 12).

Born with a full head of naturally black hair, Anderson had been interested in acting and public performance since she was a child. At age ten she played an Indian princess in her first of many school plays (Hoover, Riley 115). As a teenager, Anderson gave her father, a wealthy

St. Paul chemist, and mother quite a time: "[I was a normal teenager until I] discovered boys," said Anderson. "My father was not pleased—the ones who liked me all seemed to have long hair and drive motorcycles" (Hoover, Riley 115).

Her first experience with marriage was a disaster. Marrying a man she had only known for three weeks—she blamed that on being on the rebound from another love affair—Anderson was divorced within three months (Hoover, Riley 115). During the brief marriage, however, Anderson became pregnant and, at 18, was a divorced mom. Though she wanted to be on her own, circumstances forced Anderson to return home to her parents, who insisted that Anderson put herself through school. "It was the greatest gift they could have given me—my independence," recalled Anderson in a 1979 interview. "I learned how to make it on my own" (Hoover, Riley 115).

Anderson studied art and obtained a teaching certificate at the University of Minnesota. She was never interested in teaching as a serious profession, but, as a single mother, she wanted a stable career to fall back on. Determined to make it in show business, Anderson, wearing a blonde wig, auditioned for and received the role of Billie in a Minneapolis repertory company's production of "Born Yesterday." From there, Anderson began working in midwestern road companies and theater groups.

It was during this time that Anderson met Ross Bickell, an actor playing the lead in the Old Log Theater production of "Play it Again, Sam." Anderson later recalled that the two fell in love at first sight. The romances was complicated, however, by the fact that Ross was seeing someone else at the time. Loni and Ross tried to fight their attraction for each other, but to no avail; in 1974, six months after they met, they were married (Torgerson 12).

The Minneapolis theater experience also brought Anderson to an interesting career decision. "I was working in a play with Pat O'Brien, who later ended up playing a role in [the *WKRP* episode "Jennifer and the Will"]," recalled Anderson. He told me, 'I think you should go to Hollywood.'

"I said, 'No, no, no, no, no—I don't want to deal with all of the competition. There are too many pretty ladies in Hollywood.'

"And Pat O'Brien said, 'True, but there aren't that many *funny* pretty ladies in Hollywood" (Anderson).

Loni and Ross moved to Hollywood in 1975. Determined to find work, but tired of playing the "exotica" her black hair dictated, Anderson became a blonde. Aware that beautiful blondes have the tendency to get cast in stereotypical roles, Anderson vowed that she would never play a "dumb blonde." The "Pretty-Funny" lady soon landed a number of roles, including guest spots on *The Bob Newhart Show* and *Three's Company*. She had not really considered taking a role in a series because she felt it would take too much time away from her family. "I never wanted fame," said Anderson. "I just wanted to be a working mom." However, after working on *The Bob Newhart Show* and *Phyllis*, Anderson thought that she would enjoy working in an MTM series; she liked their style (Torgerson 12).

Anderson first learned of the Jennifer Marlowe role from her husband, who had auditioned for the part of Andy Travis. It is here where the stories of Anderson's landing the role—or, rather, the story of the conditions of her accepting the role—conflict. Claiming that the original script portrayed Jennifer as a typical dumb blonde, Anderson insists that the sexy-smart receptionist was her idea.

According to various interviews Anderson has done since 1979, Ross came home with a copy of the *WKRP* script and told Anderson that there was a part in it for a blonde. Ross added that he felt she would not want to take it; Anderson agreed. However, according to Anderson, Wilson and Grant Tinker wanted her for the part. "Hugh and Grant wanted me for weeks to read for the part, but I was convinced that it was a window-dressing dumb blonde part," said Anderson. "For three weeks they kept after me to read for the role. I was doing an episode of *The Incredible Hulk* at the time and I couldn't get away during the week. Hugh and Grant agreed to come in on a Saturday to hear me read for the role. I figured that if they were willing to go that far, the least I could do was stop in, but I was going to make it clear that I was not the least bit interested in playing a dumb blonde (Anderson).

"When that Saturday came, I did exactly as I had planned to do. I drove down there and gave my speech to Grant and Hugh, saying that the way the character was in the script was not the way I would do the role. Grant Tinker then asked me, 'Well, how would you do it?'

"I said, 'I think I'd like to look at it like Lana Turner would look at the role, and do it that way.' Apparently he and Hugh were impressed, and by Monday we were making arrangements [for me to take the role]" (Anderson).

Hugh Wilson tells a different story: "Well, you know, Loni, she'd do interviews and she'd say, 'I told them, I made sure I wasn't going to play a dumb blonde.' We would always let her do that, play that out—hell, they're not interviewing me anyhow—but [Jennifer] was never [to be] a dumb blonde. That was in the plans right from the beginning" (Wilson).

While other actors and writers who were privy to that first script concur with Wilson's version of the story, it is difficult to say with certainty which version is the most accurate. First of all, one must consider Anderson's background, which included a history of sexy/smart blondes—even in her appearance on *Three's Company*, a show not noted for its fairness to women. Also, Anderson is quick to point out that she had agreed to do a "ditzy" blonde role in another pilot for CBS. Finally, it is possible that, from the sparsity of lines given Jennifer in the pilot script, Anderson may have truly believed the character was a dumb blonde—thus, the two versions of the story may simply come down to a matter of different perceptions of the same material.

Another point to ponder is the significant yet subtle Jennifer Marlowe character change that took place after the first episode. In the first scene in the pilot, Jennifer referred to station manager Arthur Carlson as "the jerk who runs this place." Faithful viewers of the show can quickly see that this was totally inconsistent with the way Jennifer dealt with or talked about Carlson in every episode after the pilot. Indeed, by the second episode, Jennifer became Carlson's most avid defender. Though this change has nothing to do with the fact that Jennifer was always a smart blonde, it does show that there was a change that took place from the first and second episodes and that the character was not fully defined at the time of the pilot.

In the long run, it is not important whose version of the story is right or wrong, but that both Anderson, through her acting, and Wilson, through his writing, were able to bring to life a character that has become an icon in American television—the first sexy/smart blonde. Regardless of who had the idea, it was ultimately up to Wilson to write it and for Anderson to pull it off. "Loni," sighed Wilson. "God, she was good I mean, she was good...If you wrote a joke, sometimes the actor couldn't do it...you'd have to throw it out or rewrite the joke or figure out another way to do it...Man, you gave Loni something and she'd just...you'd pitch it, and she'd hit it...way out in the field somewhere—homerun" (Wilson).

Anderson is equally quick to credit Wilson for his contribution to the role. "I always liked working with Hugh and I always found it so wonderful that he was able to write such great things for my character. I loved Jennifer and I would love to be like her, but I don't have great writers in my personal life to write such wonderful lines as those written for Jennifer" (Anderson).

Though Jennifer Marlowe told viewers over and over again that she was a smart blonde, Anderson often found herself in the unfortunate position of having to defend herself to the critics. For every kind word the press would have, there would be those accompanying snide comments lambasting Loni for her beauty. As will be discussed later, many of the problems the critics had were not so much because of Anderson, but because of their own warped perceptions of American culture. Nevertheless, much of the negative criticism is unfair to both Wilson, who gave us the character, and to Anderson, who has proven time and again that her looks are secondary to her talent.

The Importance of "Home Training"
Tim Reid

Tim Reid has always been aware of the responsibility that a black actor has to his community. Therefore, he tries to make sure that blacks are reflected accurately in all the work that he does. This was a concern for Reid even in *WKRP*; he wanted to make sure that Venus Flytrap would have the opportunity to grow into a more fully developed character.

"In any kind of work I've ever done, I've always tried to put, for want of a better word, my 'home training' into my work," said Reid. "I come from a proud and vibrant black community, and my family [was]...very interwoven into the community, the church,—everything...So, whenever I approach my work and I see what I know is wrong, like depictions of say, my heritage, red flags go up and either I go, 'I can't do this,' or, 'I'm going to try to get into it [in hopes of solving the problems].'"

Part of Reid's home training involved a family life that, while financially under-privileged, was rich with love. Born in Norfolk, Virginia, Reid recalls that his family did a lot of moving, "especially around the time the rent was due." Some of these moves took Reid to Baltimore and Nashville. However, at nine, he moved back to Norfolk to live with his grandmother. "Nothing tragic about it," comments Reid "We've always been a close family and my grandmother and I loved each other very much. That cliche about all a child needs is love is true."

Reid developed an interest in the movies. He remembers staying up nights with his grandmother to watch the late shows, where he would marvel not only at the actors, but at the whole creative process. "I loved movies, but I never wanted to be an actor. I've never dreamt of just being an actor. I always dreamt of being a creative person, and acting is just a vehicle for me to do what I truly want to do, which is to produce and create movies and television."

His early life was not without its problems. During his teens, Reid became involved with local gangs and began performing poorly in school. Deciding that his son required a firm hand, Reid's father, living in Chesapeake, Virginia, sent for his son. The discipline worked, and Reid became a valued member of his school track team, was elected vice-president of the student council, and served as editor of his yearbook.

Although Reid considered joining the Air Force after high school, he and a friend ended up in the affluent Virginia Beach area where Reid landed a job waiting tables at a posh April-thru-December restaurant. Working hard, Reid earned enough money to attend Norfolk State College, an all-black school. In his junior year, his drama professor strongly encouraged Reid to read for a part in "Oedipus Rex." Reid landed the role and further developed his interest in theater. That same year, Reid, a business marketing major, got the opportunity to join the Corporate Management Training Program at DuPont. The only black selected that season for the new program, Reid took the offer, which guaranteed him a job upon graduation. Degree in hand, Reid moved to Chicago, where he became a DuPont marketing representative serving three midwestern states.

In Chicago, Reid met Tom Dressen, an insurance agent-turned-comedian. Discovering they had similar ambitions, the two formed a friendship that developed into a partnership. Together, they developed a humorous anti-drug presentation that they performed for local grade schools. After gaining Jaycee sponsorship, the duo began performing for other groups around the Windy City. Six weeks after their first presentation, they found themselves playing in a small club outside Chicago. "One person laughed and we were hooked," recalls Reid. Billed as "Tim and Tom," they landed a spot in Jesse Jackson's first Black Expo in Chicago. "We followed Stevie Wonder, who got a standing ovation," remembered Reid. "We played to 60,000 people—as they were leaving."

Within six months, Tim and Tom were a hit, making the talk show circuit with appearances on shows hosted by Merv Griffin and David Frost. The team decided to call it quits in 1975, and Reid began a solo career. Working as Della Reese's opening act, Reid captured a recurring role on the CBS summer replacement series *Easy Does It*. From there he made guest appearances on *Rhoda, Lou Grant, Maude, Fernwood 2-Night*, and *What's Happening*. He also had a recurring role on *The Richard Pryor Show*.

With experience under his belt, Reid, along with several other actors, went off to audition for the part of Venus Flytrap. "...It was more personality than based on talent," remembered Reid, "because the others certainly were as talented or more talented than myself. It's just that my view of the future of the project seemed to interest Hugh Wilson...

"...I went in and literally almost turned [Hugh] down because I was afraid of being a character named Venus Flytrap. The character in the pilot was a bit shallow and on the broad side and I just didn't want to play another stereotypical black character. I was having one of those days where you say what's on your mind, which is against Hollywood policy,—when you audition for parts you never tell them what you think of the material...I've done that since then and have been fired, and in other instances not gotten the part.

"Well, in this particular case, I just felt like telling him how I felt...It surprised Hugh, I think, and he said 'Well that's nice to know, I hadn't considered anything like that...I agree with you that this character should be more than one dimensional—he should have a human side to him—but right now we're doing a pilot. If we go to series, I would hope that whoever had the part was looking in that direction and could bring something to the character' " (Reid).

Wilson was grateful for Reid's input. "I wanted to have a black DJ, and he hardly appears in the pilot, he just comes in at the end...I use him really as a stage device to scare the hell out of [Momma] Carlson...then Timmy and I...sat down and really talked the thing over and he decided that he would rather play away from the street black. I immediately agreed with him on that. So his character—he shows up in a wild outfit —...began to change quite rapidly."

Indeed, while Wilson had definite ideas about many of the characters like Carlson or Johnny Fever, he let Reid take the lead in creating Venus. "Reid...being a black man and knowing more about being a black man than I would ever presume to guess, I more or less let him take the character..." (Wilson).

This was welcome news to Reid, who did, indeed, put his home training into the role. While it was not until the end of the first season that Reid's character began to be developed, by the end of the four-year series run, Venus Flytrap was anything but a stereotypical role. Provided with many excellent scripts, some of which he wrote himself, Reid took a two-dimensional "stage device" and turned him into a real, three-dimensional person.

Cover Girl Makes Good
Jan Smithers

It was strictly by chance that Jan Smithers became an actress. In 1966, when America was desperately trying to figure out what made teenagers tick, *Newsweek* did a cover story on the subject. Claiming to have employed every journalistic tool available, the massive study, which included interviews with close to 1,000 representative American teens, culminated in an 18-page article that looked at the attitudes, culture, desires and fads of young Americans. Singled out for the article's close-up section "Six Faces of Youth," Smithers appeared on the cover of the March 21, 1966 *Newsweek*.

Smithers's bright face, which peered back over her shoulder as she rode astride a motorcycle, was fresh and tantalizing, inviting the readers to spend the 40 cents to find out what was going on with her generation. Inside, the copy read, "Blonde and copper-toned, 16-year-old Jan Smithers of Woodland Hills, a section of Los Angeles, orbits between the world of the Surf and the Strip. At Malibu Beach she and the other bikini-clad 'golden girls' take their places in the sun, switch on their transistors and lie back to watch the members of the Malibu Surfing Association riding the 10-foot 'curls' into the shore" ("Six Faces" 66).

Reflecting on the story in a 1980 *TV Guide* interview, Smithers admitted that, before the *Newsweek* cover, she had hardly ever got out to the beach and that she had never been on a motorcycle (Esterly, "I Felt..." 12).

In fairness to Newsweek, the article did mention Smithers' domestic side: "The chatter seems to support the Hollywood version of teenage life in Southern California as one long beach party. But the scene, like a picture of Jan herself, is provocative but misleading. The swinging parties are usually held by older youths and, although 16-year-olds like Jan sometimes are invited by college friends, mostly they stick to homework and TV" ("Six Faces" 66).

Smithers was a very introspective child, concerned about the problems affecting the world. "Sometimes when I'm sitting in my room I just feel like screaming and pounding my pillow," Smithers told *Newsweek*. Smithers went on to say in the article that she was very confused about the world and what was happening ("Six Faces" 66).

Much like Bailey Quarters, Smithers was also very interested in social and political issues. In a 1980 *TV Guide* article, Smither revealed that she had always been sensitive to world and political problems; at the age of five she recalled being terrified of the bomb. "My mother told me that's when I became introverted," said Smithers, who felt that the world could not be trusted" (Esterly, "I Felt..." 14).

Smithers' early life was no beach party. Two weeks before the *Newsweek* article hit the stands, her parents had been divorced and Smithers and her three sisters were moved about between their parent's homes. Smithers, who often felt like dropping out of high school, met with another tragedy. After three attempts at understanding geometry, Smithers finally passed the course. Racing home to tell her mother the news, Smithers' car swerved and plowed into a telephone pole. She suffered a broken jaw and was left with a scar on her chin. As Smithers lay in the emergency room awaiting treatment, she was very hurt by an insensitive comment uttered by one of the attending nurses: "Oh, too bad —she used to be such a pretty girl" (Esterly, "I Felt..." 12).

In the *Newsweek* article, Smithers admitted that after her accident she went back to an old boyfriend. She was worried that she had become ugly and wanted to make sure she had somebody. This low self-esteem led her to believe that other negative things would continue to happen to her (Esterly, "I Felt..." 12).

Other "negative things" followed: One of her sisters was killed in a car wreck. Shortly after that, her mother died. Feeling adrift and alone —never able to communicate with her lawyer father—Smithers was on the verge of buckling. Trying to pull herself out, Smithers, according to *TV Guide*, accepted some TV commercials offered as a result of the *Newsweek* cover. Though she admitted being nervous in those early situations, she forced herself to continue. Smithers also began studying art at the California Institute of the Arts (Esterly, "I Felt..." 12).

At 19, Smithers decided to become a professional actress. Though she lost some roles because of her scar, Smithers persevered. She studied acting, started doing more commercials, and eventually began earning some film credits as well. She appeared in *Where the Lilies Bloom* and *Our Winning Season*. In 1978, she auditioned for the part of Bailey Quarters. Wilson had very definite ideas about the role. He had patterned Bailey after his own wife, whom he described as "very shy, but very smart—the sort of person people tend to dismiss as a jerk until they find out she's got so much to offer" (Esterly, "I Felt..." 13).

Something in Smithers' personality touched Wilson's vision of the character. "...other actresses read better for the part, but they were playing shy," said Wilson. "Jan was shy." As had happened with Gordon Jump, Smithers was immediately awarded the role (Esterly, "I Felt..." 13).

"The Strangest Audition I Was Ever to Have"
Richard Sanders

Richard Sanders had been interested in acting ever since he was a kid. The son of an Army lieutenant colonel, Sanders showed his flair for performance in many ways, whether he was being the class clown, acting out scenes from movies with his older brother at home, or appearing in productions at his Leavenworth, Kansas high school theater. Michael Fairman, Richard's friend and writing partner, speculated that acting may have been Sanders' way of escaping from his father's discipline (Esterly, "Being..." 46).

After graduating as valedictorian of his class in 1958, Sanders attended Carnegie Tech, now Carnegie-Mellon, in Pittsburgh. "They had an acting major," recalls Sanders. "...At the time, Northwestern had a drama department, but I think Carnegie Tech was the first college where you could major in theater. Most of our classes were in rehearsal and performance" (Sanders).

From there, Sanders received a Fulbright scholarship and went on to study at the London Academy of Music and Dramatic Art. Upon his return to the States, riding on the results of such impressive accomplishments, Sanders found work in local repertory theater companies.

Though it would be hard to imagine Les Nessman as a member of the Peace Corps—such a thing could spell the end of diplomatic relations as we know them—in 1966, Sanders decided to see more of the world and joined the organization. Sanders and his wife, whom he has since divorced, were assigned to Pariaba, Brazil, where his assignment was to teach acting. "[It's] kind of strange to teach acting in the Peace Corps. I directed plays, I got involved in the community, and therefore I wasn't seen as a threat. I wasn't sent there to spy" (Sanders).

Convincing the people of the community of his benign role, however, was not always easy. "One of my students told me once what a great teacher I was," recalled Sanders in a 1981 *TV Guide* interview. "Then he pulled out a pistol, put it on the table and said, 'But if the revolution comes, you'll be the first to go' " (Esterly, "Being..." 47).

Sanders found his Peace Corps experience to be as valuable as his four years at Carnegie Tech (Esterly, "Being..." 47). After returning from Brazil, Sanders began working regularly at the Arena Stage in Washington, D.C. He also performed on Broadway as the only white actor in the otherwise black cast of "Raisin," a musical version of "A Raisin in the Sun" (Sanders). Coming out to California on vacation, Sanders began to find work in episodic series and TV movies. His first guest appearance was in an episode of *McCloud*, in which he played an I.R.A. terrorist. Sanders' other characters included psychopaths and Nazis. He also appeared in the movies *Alexander: The Other Side of Dawn, Good Against Evil, Ruby and Oswald, and Keefer* (Esterly, "Being..." 47).

Sanders' work in Los Angeles theater led to his landing the Les Nessman role. Appearing as James Joyce in the play "Travesties," Sanders impressed *WKRP*'s casting director. "[He] ...told Hugh that if I could do that role, I should be able to do almost anything—it was a very strange play," said Sanders.

Sanders read for Wilson. After Wilson felt confident in Sanders' ability, he sent the actor on to read for the network. Sanders was surprised and a little intimidated by the group, which consisted of 15 people sitting around a large table. "[That was] the strangest audition I was ever to have," said Sanders. "I had no idea what that was about. I met the head of comedy at CBS. The head of comedy—you'd think he'd come out...wearing a court jester suit or something. He said that he had to have those people hear me read just to justify their jobs."

Sanders created part of the Les Nessman character during the casting process. Before reading for the role, Sanders found some old glasses—his high school glasses from the 1950s—in his briefcase. "They were perfect for Les, and, so, I adapted them."

After landing the role, Sanders decided to do some research, which included a visit to KMWB, an all-news operation in L.A. The station, however, was "too modern" to be of any use to his character. Sanders, who had worked at the school radio station at Carnegie-Tech, called on that experience to help him define his new character. "It was a very rinky-dink station," recalled Sanders. "We had a very bad board and none of us at the station really knew what we were doing. That was more typical of *WKRP* and I could think back to that experience..." (Sanders).

Join the Navy—See Hollywood
Frank Bonner

Though Frank Bonner had never worked in radio, his rank in the Navy was "Radioman Second-Class." Those who believe in fate could say it was a foreshadowing of roles to come—after all, Herb Tarlek was sort of a "second-class radio man" himself. It was Bonner's love of acting that helped him decide to join the Navy; a recruiter promised that Bonner would be stationed at San Diego Harbor, close to Los Angeles. After a few years in Hawaii, the Philippines, Japan, China, and Midway Island, Bonner wondered if his dream of seeing L.A. would ever be realized. "Only during the last year, when I finally was stationed in San Diego Harbor, did I get to drive to Los Angeles on the weekends," says Bonner. "Mostly, I saw plays and talked to actors. I was trying to prepare myself."

Bonner's preparation for a career in show business began much earlier than that; his mother and father were both performers. His father not only played with legendary musicians such as Harry James and Tommy Dorsey, but had also led his own dance orchestra. "He was a sax man and met my mother when she was a band singer," said Bonner.

Bonner was born in Little Rock, Arkansas and graduated from high school in Malvern, Texas. After his stint in the Navy, Bonner decided to stay in Hollywood, supporting himself by rebuilding car engines and working as a paralegal. After a hard day's work, Bonner would work evenings in community theater. "Wherever there was an audition, I was there." Bonner received a number of roles in which he had the chance to prove his talent was as great as his desire. In one play, "The Child Buyer," Bonner played a 14-year-old. In "The Lesson," Bonner played an ancient professor. This versatility impressed director Ed Ludlum, who was directing the play "The Only Bathtub in Cassis." When Bill Bixby, the original choice for the role, became unavailable, Bonner got the part.

More stage roles followed, including "The Sign in Sidney Brustein's Window," for which Bonner won the first acting award ever presented by the Los Angeles critic's circle. Bonner also guested on *The Young Lawyers, The FBI, Mannix, Love American Style, Emergency,* and *Police Woman.* Bonner was playing the lead in David Storey's "In Celebration" at the Company of the Angeles Theater when he was spotted by casting director Bob Manahan and asked to read for the part of Herb Tarlek. However, this did not mean Bonner was a shoe-in for the role.

"As Hollywood usually goes," recalls Bonner, "there is a great deal of luck involved and that's what was involved when I landed the role of Herb. I say that because I was, like, third choice in casting. The story I like to tell—which people are generally aghast at—is the fact that Howard Hesseman was the first choice for the role of Herb."

When Hesseman refused to play Tarlek, Bonner became one of several actors considered. "...It came down to me and a very good friend of mine, Rod McCarey. And they said, 'Well, let's go with Rod.' he had a track record—he was coming off of *General Hospital* and I was coming off of a day here on *Mannix* and a day there on *The FBI*...and a lot of commercials—nothing really heavyweight—So, they said, 'Okay. Rod's the man.'

"Well, Rod, in the meantime, goes across town to read for another pilot called *Mother, Jugs and Speed* and gets that, as well. Here Rod is, sitting on two pilots and having to make a choice. He said he literally flipped a coin and it came down heads, which meant *Mother, Jugs, and Speed.* Probably he thought that *WKRP* wouldn't go. Like I say, it's all a crap shoot—you never know.

"So, [Rod] took *Mother, Jugs and Speed*, which never saw the light of day, and MTM went with their third choice, which was Frank Bonner."

Bonner wasn't the only character to find himself second or third on the list. "I think, out of the eight characters on *WKRP*, with the exception of maybe two—Jan Smithers...and Richard Sanders—everyone else were all second and third choices in casting."

Herb was a test character, which meant that Bonner was signed to seven out of the original 13 episodes ordered by the network. "I knew I was just going to have to fight like crazy to find something with this guy to make him work." According to Bonner, the original concept of Herb had nothing to do with the wardrobe, although Wilson has suggested that Clark Brown, the character upon which Herb was based, did dress in a similar fashion. However, by looking at the pilot, Bonner's story holds up—he is relatively color coordinated. "Nothing outlandish," said Bonner. "As I recall, I'm in pretty much basic blues.

"The ultimate character breakdown of Herb was 'Six-feet-two, chiseled featured good looking guy who was an honest to goodness woman killer, but he just came on so strong that he just turned women off'." The description also called for Herb to wear three-piece suits. Bonner continued: "I remember one sentence distinctly saying, 'Herb's idea of flash is a pinkie ring that he wears,' so, that was as loud as it got, physically, from the character breakdown.

"I thought, 'Well, I'm not the six-foot, chiseled featured lady killer type—I've got troubles—I'm more a character type than I am a leading man....I said, 'Where is it? It's got to be somewhere'." By the taping of the pilot, Bonner would discover the "somewhere" in which the "it" existed, making Herb a permanent, valuable part of the show (Bonner).

Chapter Three
"Hugh's Baby"
The Pilot

Casting was not the only thing on Hugh Wilson's mind; he was also busy with his new staff of writers. Wilson, along with Tom Chehak, Blake Hunter and Bill Dial, began putting the finishing touches on the pilot script. While the staff made contributions, they are quick to point out that this was Hugh's baby.

"We were just there more as sort of the supportive crew of the pilot," said Chehak. "I think I had one joke in the pilot, Dial had three or four, and Blake probably had one or two—but the rest was all Hugh's" (Chehak).

"During production," added Hunter, "...a lot of rewriting goes on...You'll be writing in a room with a group of people and you'll be going through, punching up, making new jokes, changing things that don't work—you start taking scenes in or out—and Hugh was at the helm, but the people in the room were contributing. That was the re-write process, but the script was definitely his" (Hunter).

Part of *WKRP*'s continuity and singularity was because of Wilson's role as "hands-on" producer. Starting with the pilot, Wilson charted a course that would last through most of the show's run—a collaborative creative effort with Wilson firmly at the helm. "I was producer and the head writer," said Wilson. "I was the daddy I guess, almost for the first two-and-a-half years...maybe for the first three seasons. I either wrote or re-wrote every script...then the fourth year, I let more and more of the other writers come into it. I was kind of out of gas, but...you look at these TV shows like, for instance, the shows at the time that were on— *Barney Miller* was definitely Danny Arnold's show....*Soap* was definitely Susan Harris'.... *MASH*, for the first few years anyway, was definitely Larry Gelbart's show...There is usually just one—sometimes two—that are the final filters. That's why I think these shows have a

35

singularity about them—and that couldn't happen if these scripts were coming in from all over the place" (Wilson).

Wilson's leadership style cannot be underestimated. Wilson had—has—the incredible ability to allow great amounts of creative input from others while maintaining his own ground and enforcing his own demands. Perhaps his greatest strength was—is—his ability to listen and learn while he talks and teaches. This rare gift made for a very rare show.

"The Bastard Son of MTM"

Though it shared a common bond with other MTM shows, *WKRP* was different in both look and content. This "bastard son of MTM," as Wilson described it, was a little louder and a little faster than its MTM siblings, in part because of its rock and roll format, in part because the show was video taped. Most MTM shows were done on film. "In tape," noted Wilson, "the medium is the message. You had to shoot a show and write a show differently for tape than for film. It's got to go faster, and it's got to be louder, because film is much more forgiving than tape. If you slow down on tape you start to look like *Days of Our Lives*. I learned that really fast" (Wilson).

The decision to go to tape was purely financial. Wilson wanted to use current popular tunes and classic rock songs in the show's soundtrack, but it would cost a great deal more money to show a record being played on film than on tape. Wilson recalled that some bright executives thought they had a viable solution: "I got into this thing where they said—the networks or MTM or someone—'Well, what we'll do, we won't play actual records, we'll play sound-alikes.'

I said, "What? That's impossible. We gotta play real records."

They said, "Well, we'll get a group [for instance that] sounds like the Beach Boys."

I said, "Aw guys, that will never work."

They said, "Well, we can't, in our budget, afford to pay the royalties on all these songs."

That's why we went to tape (Wilson).

The MTM studios were not yet equipped to handle video production. Thus, Wilson and crew found themselves at Goldenwest Videotape Division—Station KTLA in Los Angeles—where the company became, as Wilson put it, an "island unto itself." Furthermore, because MTM was heavily involved with Mary Tyler Moore's new show, *The Mary Tyler Moore Comedy Hour*, no one, according to Wilson, really paid much attention to what was going on with *WKRP*. After the pilot aired, some MTM executives were surprised. " 'Jesus'," they said, recalled Wilson, " 'this doesn't look like an MTM show!' "

"The Nightmare of the Nipples"

Hollywood's pilot season begins in early spring. In March 1978, after eight days of rehearsal, the cast taped the pilot (Graham). The first characters we encountered in that episode were Herb Tarlek and Jennifer Marlowe. In what was to become a familiar scene over the next four seasons, Herb, the married sales manager who calls himself "Mr. Kickback," began hitting on Jennifer, the stunningly sexy receptionist. It is interesting to note that, with very little dialogue, Wilson was able to create great characterization and conflict. Not only did he give us a handle on Herb, but he also proved that Jennifer was no dumb blonde willing to fall for such tantalizing Tarlek offerings as "a side of beef fully dressed." Indeed, while TV critics would later blame *WKRP*'s forced mid-first season hiatus in part on Jennifer's dumb blonde image, nothing could have been further from the truth; neither in voice nor in character did Jennifer fit the stereotype. While provocative and sexy, she was also nobody's fool, least of all Herb Tarlek's (Wilson, *Pilot*).

Jennifer was almost a little too provocative for the pilot. "I got all flustered...when we went to shoot the pilot," recalled Wilson. "I'm as intimidated by a good looking woman as the next guy...so we go to tape this thing and I forget what Loni's wearing—whether she's wearing a sweater or a kind of a flimsy material dress—I forget what it was....And, you know, what they do with all that tape equipment there, they'd run the air conditioner way the hell up. And it'd be cold. And, so, we started to do the first scene and her nipples were like blasting out of this dress—the live audience was there.

"I, of course, I'm the producer, right, so they say 'We gotta' reshoot that scene. There's somebody in CBS from Standards and Practices.'

"I had noticed the nipples too, you know—my God...So they get me backstage and they wanna' know what I'm gonna' do about it—you know, like I'd know? You're always, as a producer or a director, getting questions where they say 'What's to do?' So, I'm back there with Loni and I—I'm turning red—and I keep staring at her forehead, talking to her...and it was decided that we'd put Band-Aids on her breasts. That was tried and you could see the Band-Aids...

"She says, 'Well, maybe it's just cause I'm going on and I'm getting excited...'

"I just remember it was like this dream—this nightmare of the nipples—and I...think what happened is we finally got her in some sort of metal bra or something, and went on with the shooting, but that was the big concern..." (Wilson).

Anderson recalls the problem with great humor, noting that "We talk about blood and guts all the time, but nipples are much more natural." Because of the studio air conditioning, Anderson was to be troubled by the nightmare of the nipples in every episode. "Someone once came up with the funniest idea I'd ever heard," added Anderson. "They thought I should wear a padded bra" (Anderson).

While appearance caused a problem for Anderson, it provided a solution for Bonner. Recall that, upon receiving the part, Bonner began looking for something that would make his seven-episode test character a viable part of the show; he found the answer in Herb's wardrobe.

"Just before we started taping," recalled Bonner, "I had on this basic blue pull over V-neck sweater, with a blue tie and shirt, I think, and blue slacks and a pair of white shoes—nothing really garish. But, one little thing I did have on was a white belt, but you couldn't see it because it was under the sweater. And I thought 'Maybe here's a little thing I can start on—maybe it's in his dress, in his clothes—maybe he has a little bad taste and he does little crazy things.'

"So, I, at the last minute, opted to tuck my sweater into my pants, which, to me is a little strange—every once in a while you'll see somebody do it—I think it's just terrible looking. And, that's what I did, so that my white belt would show. And my shoes matched. I thought, 'Maybe that's it. I'll always wear this white belt and shoes with everything.' That's kind of how it started and Hugh Wilson...said 'Yeah, that's funny.'

"So, that's the way they went...we went toward the clothes. And, of course, as you can tell, it really went overboard in some instances, but—it worked. People loved it. It worked...instead of doing 7 out of 13, I wound up doing 20 out of the 22 we did the first season. So, I said, 'Okay. I found it. I'm home' " (Bonner).

"The Stranger as Guide"

With Jennifer and Herb established, the pilot turned toward explaining the premise of the series. Again being economical with dialogue, Wilson was able to do this with the introduction of Andy Travis, the new program director fresh from Sante Fe, New Mexico. "...That's usually a good way to do a situation comedy pilot," commented Wilson. "It's sort of what you call 'the stranger as guide'...If a new person is brought in, then it allows me to handle exposition—He's gotta be introduced to everyone. So therefore, exposition is not shoehorned. As he finds out, the audience finds out. He becomes the audience, in a way. We are his eyes and ears. We learn as he learns. It's a good way of doing exposition without being clumsy" (Wilson).

In that first scene, Andy quickly realized that he may have made a mistake in coming to WKRP. Herb, upset that he had been passed over for the job of program director, quickly gave Travis the brush. Les Nessman gleefully warned Andy that station manager Arthur Carlson— "The Big Guy"—had a habit of quickly firing new Program Directors. All in all, it was a less-than-promising welcome (Wilson, *Pilot*).

"Grant Tinker...Was Getting Very Pale"

A careful viewing of that first scene will reveal Les Nessman's bandaged forehead. While a bandage would become a staple part of Les' wardrobe—he wore one in every episode—it's original appearance in the pilot was quite by accident. "It was about an hour before we were going to shoot the pilot," recalled Richard Sanders. "And, this light had come down from the stage—this light that had, you know, the barn doors on it. And it gashed me right in the head.

"They took me off to emergency—to the hospital. The Doctor came in and looked at it and he said that it would need stitches. We couldn't do that, and I said, 'Couldn't we just put a butterfly bandage on it?' and he said 'Yes,' but he didn't think it would hold.

"We didn't have much time. I recall that Grant Tinker was there for the pilot and he was getting very pale when we left...

"So we came rushing back to the studio and I really wanted to get on with shooting the show. I thought we could just put a bandage on it or just put on make-up, but, it turns out that with make-up it would have gotten infected.

"So they decided to put a big bandage on for the beginning and then a smaller bandage on with the passage of time in the show. They were going to put a line in to explain it—they did put a line in to explain it—but later they just took it out. The line was really silly—they had just come up with it on the spot. Therefore, it was left unexplained why this guy had this bandage.

"The show got picked up. I thought the bandage showed that the guy was kind of a klutz, so I put a bandage on for each episode. Sometimes it's pretty evident—his whole arm is gauzed up. Other times it was a very subtle bandage. There was one lady who wrote me. She'd noticed that I always had bandages on and wondered if I had boils or something.

"I remember I was just trying, the week before, to make sure that I didn't put the bandage in the same place. We were starting to run out of places to put them. I thought we'd have to do the European version—have the shirt off, or something like that."

Les' bow-tie was also an accident of sorts. "In promoting the show, we had a photo session, and I had a regular straight tie on," recalled Sanders. "One of the cameramen—one of the people doing the photo session—said, 'Try this tie.' And he had a bow tie. And that was the birth of the bow tie" (Sanders).

Of a less external nature was the bond between Herb and Les that was established in the pilot. As the series developed, this bond was enhanced to show the dichotomy of their relationship; they were best friends who jumped at the chance to cut each other's throats. "...Each one could be the butt of the other's joke," explained Bonner, "because everyone else was a little too clever—too intelligent—to pull anything on. I think they needed each other, from that stand-point...it was like a love/hate relationship." In an episode that took place a couple of seasons later, Carlson offered one of the best descriptions of Les and Herb's friendship: "You two guys are best friends, but—deep down—don't you really hate each other?" (Sanders, Fairman).

"The Characters Start Telling You Who They Are"

No matter how well defined the original character concepts may be, actors, by nature, quickly develop ideas of their own as they bring their characters to life. On *WKRP*, this was not limited to Herb's clothing or Les' bandages. Gordon Jump, who had his own experience in broadcasting, also brought his own ideas to the role. "The people that I based my character on," said Jump, "were three managers in broadcasting that I had worked for, which gave me three different facets of Arthur Carlson's personality—along with the wonderful writing of Hugh Wilson.

"Two were station managers; one was a station manager that was very autonomous in his running of his station. When he came up with an idea, it was, 'That's the way were gonna' do it, and I expect you to get behind it—don't give me any excuses, let's just get the job done.' [He did it] with that blustery attitude.

"...And the other man was a very gentle man who was a manager by your commitment. He would come into your office and say, 'What do you see us doing out of this office say for the next six months?.'

"And you would say, 'Well, I'd like to do so and so and so and so....'

"And he'd say, 'Well, that sounds like a good idea. When do you think you can have that ready?' And this was the type of manager that he was—he was a wonderful man. That was the gentler, I think more lovable, quality of Arthur Carlson.

"...The other [a station sales manager,] was sort of a pompous guy. And, he dealt with the station rep in New York and he was a very funny man to me because he was so full of cliches—sort of like, 'We're gonna' throw this thing on the wall and see if it sticks.' That sort of approach. Very colorful and pompous" (Jump).

Wilson considered such contributions to be a necessary and inevitable part of the total creative process. "The characters were there and I had a pretty definite idea of what I wanted," said Wilson. "What happens is, when an actor begins to say the lines, it begins to come alive and then things begin to change, because it's not precisely what you had in mind, right? An actor brings a lot to it...

"[This sort of thing happens with] even the sets...You had the sets built, and you say, 'Oh, that looks a little different than what I thought—it's not wrong, it's just different.' You know, so your ideas begin to change—this is what always happens. The head writer—myself—creates these characters, then the actors breath life into them and then you begin to chase the characters. You go down the stage everyday and watch rehearsals and you get ideas and the characters start telling you who they are, rather than you telling them who they are" (Wilson).

Howard Hesseman, who had worked as a DJ, also had his own ideas about his character; this often caused friction between Hesseman and Wilson. To Wilson, Fever was Skinny Bobby Harper. Hesseman, however, had no history with Skinny Bobby; he had role models of his own. "[Skinny Bobby] was, you know...another disk jockey," explained Hesseman. "He was a nice guy and he was an old friend of Hugh's, but I can't remember very much about him. He and Hugh were friends, so Hugh had real ideas about the character based on his experience with this guy, but—I don't know this guy, I don't have any experience with him, so I'm looking at a text, I'm looking at a script—words on paper—and I have my own ideas based on my own experience and my imagination.

"So, I'm drawing on my experiences, my relationships with radio people, and my imagination as an actor. And that vision of this character was not always totally in line with the vision that Hugh had. But, it seemed to me that what we were always ultimately going for was some synthesis—some version—that would be satisfactory for both of us" (Hesseman).

Despite the occasional conflicting interpretations—or, perhaps, because of them— Fever emerged as one of the pilot's most well defined characters. Armed with great lines, along with actions that spoke louder than words, Hesseman painted Fever as a paranoid insomniac who had been, over the years, bounced around from town to town. In creating an almost physical blur of a person, Hesseman was able to bring to life the flurry of a radio career that took Fever from a $100,000 a year job in L.A. to an underpaid stint as the host of a garden show in Amarillo, Texas (Wilson, *Pilot*).

Hesseman's most brilliant moment in the pilot—a scene that *The Wall Street Journal* said stole the show (Graham)—occurred when Fever broke the new rock and roll format. "I wrote that, actually, about two days before we shot it, with Jack Riley, who did the warm-up for the pilot show," recalled Hesseman. "Jack Riley used to play Mr. Carlin on the old *Bob Newhart* show. They brought Jack in to do the warm-up and we went out for lunch and I was noodling stuff for Fever's raps and we started playing with all of those physician, medical allusions. You know, the 'Big musical medicine cabinet, 25,000 watts of healing—the healing prescription.' Yeah, whatever all that riff was. Jack and I were writing that at lunch.

"That was one thing that I got right away early in the pilot rehearsals—that Hugh was basically not opposed to my riffing and improvising...many of the scripts, which I still have in storage somewhere, just say, 'Act one, scene two—cut to booth. Johnny is cuing record. Johnny intros record—to come.'

"So it was up to me, and I would do it based on a record I had chosen. I would do a little work at home with my own turntable—just working out pieces of business with the board so I could practice the rap...because when I was doing it in front of an audience I was trying to do it right" (Hesseman).

"TV's First Prime Time Pot Head"

Fever became an important, ground breaking character. He was the sort of person that television had spent 25 years warning us against—a paranoid under-achiever (12 years before Bart Simpson) who admitted in the pilot that hogs have more of a future than he does. A 1970 version of Maynard G. Krebs, Fever was more than a social misfit. In a way, he was what Fonzie of *Happy Days* could have been, had not the *Happy Day*'s producers opted to make Fonzie a clean-cut role model. One could think of Fever as the adult prototype of Bart Simpson.

Part of Fever's singularity came from his almost unabashed use of recreational drugs. Indeed, Hesseman likes to describe the DJ as "TV's first prime time pot-head." Yet there was more to Fever than his neurosis and occasional drug use. "...As an actor," said Hesseman, "it was important to me to show that, simply because he was using soft drugs, he was still a responsible human being who understood loyalty between friends, who understood responsibilities of employment, who understood social responsibilities, and whose life also reflected a series of failures—fuck-ups—that may or may not be attributable, to some degree, to his use of soft drugs. But, I thought the fact that he was a pot head was just one aspect of his personality.

"...It seemed to me on some level you could say, 'Okay, this character does have what it takes to extricate himself from what he perceives to be less than he deserves. A lesser setting than he deserves. He does have the talent. He has the commitment. He does have all of that.' But, in fact, he likes being there. It is comfortable. It is a comfortable hammock between the kind of support that he's going to get from Travis and Venus and the other jocks and the two women, and the kind of healthy antagonistic energy that he's gonna' be able to get off of Tarlek and Nessman and Carlson" (Hesseman).

Hesseman scoffs at the notion that the DJ was lovable. "I appreciate that people liked him, but a lot of times he had a very sour, passive, cynical approach to life that conceivably could be a turn-off for a lot of people, particularly in the 1980s, what with Reaganism and that mindless optimism," commented Hesseman. "I mean, I don't have a lot of trouble with cynicism myself—but, I just thought that he was a character that—I don't know—he seemed like a human guy to me—I wanted to keep him human" (Hesseman).

Hesseman is quick to point out that the show's music also provided a great deal of support to Fever. Programming most of his own music— Tim Reid programmed his own, as well—Hesseman tried to find various rock tunes that would either effect a certain emotion or enhance a particular action. "Plato says, 'Music and rhythm find their way to the secret places of man's soul,'" quotes Hesseman. "I mean, here's a guy who deals with music all of the time. Thus, a great deal of his life is not simply infused with music and informed by it, but he's passing that on to other people.

"In the context of the show, I had the opportunity to interact— sometimes solo—with the music. I didn't have to be talking with someone else to make a joke. I could be talking about a piece of music or I could be listening to a piece of music and let it score the scene or suggest the mood or counterpoint what was going on. That was the great fun of choosing the music each week" (Hesseman).

Hesseman's choices clearly showed that Fever was a rock and roll purist. To Fever, an appreciation of the classics meant listening to Chuck Berry and Bo Diddley. This was an interesting counterpoint to the dwindling-but-still-present disco scene of the late 1970s and early 1980s. Furthermore, while Fever considered disco a disease worse than the plague, he was also reluctant to play top-40 rock. "I thought Fever's taste was under the gun all the time," said Hesseman. "That he was trying to be a part of a commercially successful operation that just wasn't making it. But he was making certain concessions to that effort" (Hesseman).

With Fever's concessions coming few and far between, the resulting tension effected a rift that complemented the one between WKRP's old and new guards; it provided comedic friction amongst the rockers themselves, particularly between Fever and Travis. Thus, when *WKRP* could not turn to a Herb-Les-Carlson vs. Travis-Bailey-Venus-Fever confrontation, it had the alternate top-40 vs. classic rock tension. This, in turn, provided more depth, realism and options to the series.

Meanwhile, Back at the Pilot...

With WKRP's rock format in place, things began to change. The shy, college educated Bailey Quarters was invited to her first meeting. Johnny Fever started enjoying his work. Even Herb and Les came around and pledged their allegiance to Andy. However, when Momma Carlson, the "mean little momma" who owned the station, became upset at the "loud music she heard emanating from her radio," Herb, Les and Carlson quickly jumped ship. After an eloquent plea to save his job, supplemented by Arthur finally standing up to his mother, Andy and Carlson finally convinced Momma to give the new format a try (Wilson, *Pilot*).

The role of Momma was given to veteran actress Sylvia Sidney, who is best known for her excellent ingenue performances in 1930 Warner Brother's films such as *Dead End*. "She was an interesting lady," recalled Jump. "I felt in the pilot she was thrown with eight people who had no track record. And, here was a brilliant star of the early days of the movies—I mean, this was an ingenue actress of great breadth and scope. Here she is, thrown in to do a television situation with eight people she's never heard of. And I'm sure that, because of the medium, she was a little taken aback. But none-the-less, she gave a wonderful performance" (Jump).

Jay Sandrich, who provided a steady hand directing the pilot, must also be given credit for the pilot's success. "We had one week," explained Jump. "And that was placed basically in the hands, of course, of Jay Sandrich, who, to my way of thinking, is a great comedy director. And Jay first of all toned me down—he said, 'Don't be so broad. You've got—if this goes—several years to let all of your little tricks out of the bag. Don't do it all in one show.'

"And, there was great input from Jay for me and I love him for it. He was honest and forthright and explicit in the direction that he gave every one of us. It was his direction, I think, in that first episode, that set the tone for the rest of the work that we would do. And, he has that marvelous ability. It was a tough week's work because we were all trying to portray characters that none of us had played before and do it in such a way that the network would take a look at the show and say, 'Hey, there's chemistry here' " (Jump).

Jay also provided a steady hand for a nervous Wilson. "I...remember throwing up," laughed Wilson. "Jay Sandrich came in and...he was a real old hand at it...he had directed many, many *Mary's*, and he was a calming influence. It was really great he was there because that live audience—the show started and I got so nervous, I walked out of the control room and went outside and threw up" (Wilson).

Testing, Testing...

Once finished, the pilot was reviewed and previewed by various audiences. "Well, we were worried, in the beginning, whether people in radio would buy it," recalled Sanders. "We had kind of a preview showing...for various people who worked in radio here in L.A.—disk jockeys and such. And they were all pretty happy. They thought we had done a realistic job, although there were things that we would do differently..." (Sanders).

Robert A. Daly, President of the CBS entertainment division, felt equally positive about the series. "I thought instantly after seeing it that this series would be on our schedule," said Daly in Graham's *Wall Street Journal* article. Daly's optimism grew stronger after the pilot tested well with sample audiences. As viewers watched the program on monitors, they expressed their approval or disapproval by pressing either a green or red button. *WKRP* passed with the proper flying colors.

"CBS really didn't know what they had," commented Jump. "When the show was done it was taken to New York. It was played before the sales moguls on Madison Avenue—the advertising people—and they stood up and gave it a standing ovation. CBS had not planned the publicity for that show at the time. They realized, 'Hey, these people are really interested in it.'

"They came back to Los Angeles and started to prepare what they needed for the press conference that had come up since they elected to use this for a fall start on television. And, when they played it before the press again, the show received a standing ovation. Friends of mine that are in the press told me that they thought it was a wonderful show. So, it was off and running" (Jump).

Despite positive reviews and good sample audience response, Arnold Becker still expressed concern over whether *WKRP* had the ability to sustain interest. Indeed, an "elevator-music-turned-rock-station story" is just a gimmick; *WKRP* needed to go beyond that, exploring the characters (Graham). Hugh and Company, of course, had every intention of going that route.

"You know," said Wilson, "you start doing these show and you say, 'There must be millions of stories about radio stations.' And, after about the fifth show, you're out of radio station stories. So, you start doing stories about the characters...the writers would all sit down and say, 'Well, who is this character, really? And what's his home-life like?' And then stories start coming out of that" (Wilson).

In May 1978, CBS commissioned 12 more episodes, for which it paid an average of $155,000 each. It was a relatively low budget, particularly during a period when prime time production was becoming increasingly expensive. Indeed, an article in *Broadcasting* magazine claimed that the networks spent, on average, 20 percent more for new programming in 1978, despite the fact that there were fewer new shows being produced that year ("Headache..." 35). Part of the low-cost per episode for *WKRP* was due to the fact that the series had no big-name stars; actor's salaries in that first season ranged from $2,000—$6,000 per episode (Graham).

What's in a Theme?

An interesting footnote to the pilot concerns *WKRP*'s closing theme. Chehak recalls how he and Wilson flew out to Cincinnati in early spring to shoot the scenes for the opening credits. After that, the two went to Atlanta to supervise Tom Welles recording of the opening theme. "Tommy did the openings," recalled Chehak. "We came to Tommy's house, and he played it on guitar for us, and Hugh loved it. And then we went over to the studio and they got all their musicians in there to lay the tracks down and somebody said, 'We gotta' have an end lick.'

"The singer who was there just started [singing nonsense lyrics]— 'blab-a-blad-a-bling-blang, blow-bling-blow.' And we said, 'That was great, let's just use it and let everybody try to figure out what they're saying.' But there's no words—nothing. That was just a little spontaneous moment...We were sitting down and it just kind of happened" (Chehak).

Of course, Welle's message in his opening lyrics ring loud and clear. A familiar ditty committed to memory by even the most passive *WKRP* fans, its allusions to "packing and unpacking up and down the dial" clearly reinforced the realism of the precarious lives of radio talent and managers.

WKRP went into production on July 20. Originally scheduled to air at 8:30 Monday night, following the new CBS magazine show *People*, *WKRP* was switched to the 8:00 lead-off position (Graham). Some may look at this last-minute change as a vote of confidence on the part of the network. Others, however, could view this change as an ominous sign of the many time slot shifts to come. Like the show's opening theme, *WKRP* often found itself "packing and unpacking, up and down the dial." And, as the song says, Hugh and Company would soon get "kind of tired" of it.

Chapter Four
"Put Us Behind *MxAxSxH*"
The First Season

The September 18, 1978 debut of *WKRP* was greeted with a fair amount of fanfare, including a number of decent reviews. *Variety* called the new series a potential hit for CBS, provided Wilson and Company could keep up the excellent writing evidenced by the pilot. Because *WKRP* was of interest to the folks in Cincinnati, *The Cincinnati Post* made quite a fuss as well.

Meet The New 'WKRP Family'
Even [Cincinnati] Mayor Springer will have to take a back seat when the new First Family comes to Cincinnati tonight.

The cast of the new CBS-TV comedy *WKRP In Cincinnati* is expected to become a familiar gang of characters in local households, according to predictions of success within the television industry. (*Cincinnati Post*)

The article, which featured a picture of the regular cast, went on to describe the format of the show. It also gave short biographical sketches of each of the actors, pointing out that both Gary Sandy and Gordon Jump were born in the Dayton, Ohio area.

Perhaps more impressive was the debut day article that appeared on the front page of *The Wall Street Journal*. Using *WKRP* as an example of how a TV show makes it to the air, the article not only spoke to the specific background of *WKRP*, but to the gestation process of sitcoms in general:

Tonight, millions of American television viewers will be formally introduced to eight people, the regular cast of the show "WKRP in Cincinnati," a new CBS comedy about a floundering radio station that switches its music format from cornball to rock.

In the television business, such first impressions are the source of all good things—namely advertising revenues and future profits. If, say, 25 million

49

viewers like the performers well enough to welcome them eagerly into their living rooms week after week, the half-hour show will be on the way to becoming a hit. As such, it could remain on the air for the next five years or more.

If, however, the elusive chemistry between viewer and performer fails to ignite, a year's effort on the part of the "WKRP" cast, as well as the network's $2 million investment in the first 13 episodes, will have been for naught. Without respectable Nielsen ratings (generally 30% of those watching TV at a given hour), the series probably will be yanked from the schedule with merciless dispatch.

...Even so, "WKRP" is more fortunate than most fledgling series. It has won raves from critics, ad agencies, and affiliated stations... (Graham)

The pilot lived up to its expectations. Airing at 8:40 pm—it was delayed by President Carter's address to Congress ("Reviews" 52)—the episode captured a 19.7 rating, being seen in 14,675,000 homes. It also scored a respectable 30 share. Unfortunately, the next seven episodes did not place as well. "Pilot Part Two," the second episode, captured only a 25 share and a dismal 15.7 rating (or 11,696,500 viewers, representing a loss of nearly 4 million viewers from the week before). This lack-luster performance continued through to November. Out of the eight episodes shown in that time period, the ratings remained in the low to mid-twenties, with the lowest rating and share—14.2 and 21, respectively—occurring on November 6. This prompted the network to temporarily remove the series from its schedule.

Various stories surfaced to explain the forced hiatus. "The highly touted *WKRP in Cincinnati,* characterized as a 'disappointment' by one CBS executive," wrote Sally Bedell in the November 11 issue of *TV Guide,* "will...be moved to another time slot to see if ratings improve" ("TV" A-4). Later, the network claimed that *WKRP* was taken off the air to give Hugh Wilson and the rest of the staff a chance to re-tool and save the show ("People Cancelled" 43). Was *WKRP* a bad show that needed revamping or were there other circumstances that contributed to its poor performance?

After looking at the early episodes, the general trends in the ratings, and the competition against which *WKRP* was set, one begins to find that the problems were not entirely the fault of the show; the main culprit was time slots. From the beginning, Wilson had argued with the network that *WKRP* was not an 8 pm "family hour" show capable of competing against NBC's strong *Little House on the Prairie* or ABC's *Monday Night Football* (which, because of time differences, was broadcast on the West Coast at 8 pm). Sizing up the competition, Gordon Jump used to say, "We're losing out to the jocks and the juveniles and the senile."

Tom Chehak recalled Wilson's frustration. "I remember Hugh coming into the office after he had a meeting with whoever was at CBS at the time, and they asked Hugh, 'What can you do to make it better?' And, Hugh said, 'Put us behind *MxAxSxH*.' That's how Hugh was" (Chehak).

Though it may have been a flip comment, Wilson's suggestion proved valid. When *WKRP* was aired behind *MASH* on October 10, the show received its highest rating—20.7—and highest share—31—to date. After *WKRP* returned on January 15, 1979, safe in its after-*MxAxSxH* 9:30 time slot, the numbers soared, with shares ranging from the low 30s to low 40s, reaching a July 9 first season high of 43. Toward the end of the first season and into the second, *WKRP* was being touted as a hit. The network said that changes in the program accounted for *WKRP*'s new found success. The TV writers believed them.

"Not a Damn Thing Changed"

It takes only a casual viewing to discover that *WKRP*, except for the subtle change in the Jennifer Marlowe character between the pilot and second episode noted in chapter two, remained the same both before and after its mid-first season hiatus. "They [say we] took the show off to revamp it," said Wilson. "I did absolutely nothing. If you look at the shows [from the initial run,] there's no revamping. They put it back on the air, gave it a better time slot and they said, 'Well, it's because they fixed the show.' But not a damn thing [changed]. We got a better time slot. It's all time slots" (Wilson).

"...The changes were changes on the part of CBS deciding where we should be," added Hesseman. "There was no real change in the tone of the show, in the approach to the story or characters—there were no real changes in terms of production—that is, how the show's were written, or how the shows were expedited. Nobody knew what those changes were, and we were never asked to implement any changes, except, you know, on a weekly basis, through [Chuck Schnable], ...who functioned as a liaison between us and CBS....[Chuck was] remarkably contributive and a 'smart cookie' in TV. I think he's one of the best network people I've ever encountered in sitcoms..." (Hesseman).

Schnable, who served as the CBS Program Executive for *WKRP* until 1980, insists that subtle changes did take place during this time period. "Originally, it was set out to have Andy Travis as the total centerpiece of the series," said Schnable, "the same way Mary was the centerpiece for *The Mary Tyler Moore Show*. And very quickly everybody realized that it was an ensemble piece like *MxAxSxH* was. So that time between November and January...was to fashion the scripts so that it became the show it did....It may have been a subtle change, but it was a definite one in its move behind *MxAxSxH*. Hugh had created such definite characters in the pilot that it was evident that it could be a *MxAxSxH*-type show" (Schanble).

To prove his point, Schnable noted a number of changes that took place after the hiatus, including the use of recurring characters such as Carol Bruce, replacing Sylvia Sidney as Momma Carlson, and Allyn Ann McLerie, who played Carlson's wife. Schnable said that these characters were added to help round out the show. Furthermore, while one pre-hiatus episode focused on Andy Travis, complete with a look at Travis' apartment and his dog Pecos Bill, the rest of the series did seem to shy away—almost awkwardly so—from developing the show's key character.

All of these changes, however, were subtle changes to which Wilson was very amenable. Furthermore, because several of the pre-hiatus episodes were devoted in large part to the development of other characters, including Les Nessman, Bailey Quarters, and Jennifer Marlowe, it is obvious that the move toward an ensemble cast was already in the works long before the network temporarily shelved the series. In reality, the only substantive changes that took place were the use of cold opens (in which a teaser precedes the title sequence) and the use of a new title sequence which replaced the inventive opening credit sequence that featured part of the theme song being played on a car radio. Even with those minor changes, however, Gary Sandy and Gordon Jump remained the only actors mentioned in the title sequence. It was not until the second season that the other actors' names were incorporated into the opening credits. Thus, while there may have been changes taking place during the hiatus, they were not the major changes the network seemed to imply.

Nevertheless, the notion that major re-tooling had occurred was taken as fact; that CBS line was perpetuated by various TV critics and writers even after the show's 1982 cancellation. TV writer Sally Bedell was convinced that one of the major changes had to do with Jennifer Marlowe. "When *WKRP* featured a witless blonde receptionist in its initial run...viewers rejected the show, [and] CBS pulled it so the producers could make some changes," wrote Bedell in her 1983 book *Up the Tube*. "The series returned and presto: The blonde had been transformed into a shrewd mother figure" (Bedell, "Up..." xvii). While convincing, Bedell's argument has one flaw—Jennifer was never portrayed as a dumb blonde.

Although this has already been discussed in reference to the pilot, the rest of the first eight episodes provide other examples of Jennifer's non-stereotypical role. Consider the October 2 episode, "Les on a Ledge," broadcast before *WKRP* was removed from the schedule. Les, accused of being a homosexual, stands on the ledge outside Carlson's office window and contemplates suicide. Amidst the hilarious furor that ensues, Jennifer and Andy are the only characters who maintain their cool. At one point, Jennifer becomes upset by Herb's unenlightened attitude toward gay people. She quickly rebuffs the salesman, saying that people have the right to lead their lives the way they want to (Wilson, "Les..."). Is this the input of a dumb blonde?

There was also "Bailey's Show," which aired on October 23. Bailey is desperately trying to find the perfect guest for her new public affairs program "Cincinnati Beat." When the guest she books turns out to be a raving lunatic, Herb, Les and Carlson go on the warpath. Jennifer consoles the beaten and down Bailey by asking her, "If you can't handle Herb, Les and 'The Big Guy,' who in this world can you handle?" Armed with that advice, Bailey stands up for her right to a second chance. Note that it is Jennifer who acts as the voice of reason—the pivotal, centering character (Armor, Neer "Bailey's Show") Quite a tall order for a "dumb blonde."

Why did Jennifer garner such a bad rep? As is the problem with many writers who try to second guess the American mind, Bedell seemingly took a network claim at face value and, without looking into the facts, generalized it to suit her own thesis. The deeper question here, from a popular culture standpoint, is why did Bedell and other TV writers go off half-cocked when all they had to do was spend four hours taking a closer look at those first eight episodes? Did Bedell and the others fall into the trap of the stereotype they felt they were uncovering? Did they merely see a pretty face and stunning body and immediately assume that the character must be an idiot?

"I find all of those people [who base things on one or two casual viewings] ridiculous—they haven't done their homework," observed Loni Anderson, who admits that she was very uncomfortable with the negative attention the role brought her.

Tim Reid, who had taken some flack from various writers for allegedly portraying a stereotypical black, has his own ideas on the matter: "[Writers would] see one or two episodes—Let's say someone tuned in to see an episode of *KRP* and maybe my character had on a big coat or a cape or something, and they would walk away thinking, 'Oh that's just another one of those stereotypical buffoon kind of characters,' whereas they never really got a full measure...they never got a full understanding.

"I read a book...written by a black doctor of the media—or I don't know what kind of a degree he had—but he took my character to task. You know, saying it was a 'Typical stereotypical, broad, flashy dressing, street-talking kind of guy.' And he was never that! We went to great lengths to give a back story on this character, where you saw all of the disguise, all of the persona of radio. When he signed off this guy went home and read the classics...I mean we went to way, way the other way with this character" (Reid).

Understanding this type of unfair treatment delivered by media historians is key to the study and history of *WKRP*. It is also important to the study of TV in general. On the one hand, it shows the critics dependence upon and acceptance of information supplied by network public relations departments. Conversely, it shows the critic's reluctance toward independent investigation. This is not to say that Bedell or other TV writers are patently irresponsible, for there were many changes going on in TV that may have given rise to such interpretations of the Jennifer Marlowe character.

The Jiggle Factor
In the late 1970s, television introduced America to a new equation—the jiggle factor, or, as it was more commonly called, T & A (for "tits

and ass"). The idea was to have a number of shows with a number of women with as much of their physical attributes squeezed into as little clothing as possible. Thus, programs such as *Charlie's Angels* (which debuted in 1976), with Farrah Fawcett at the fore, and *Three's Company* (which debuted in 1977) with Suzanne Somers, began to grace American screens. Ignoring that women could have any more sense than a sense of revealing fashion, programs like these brought critical clamor from television critics and social scientists.

Tim Brooks and Earl Marsh, in their *Directory to Prime Time Network TV Show*'s review of *Charlie's Angels*, helped to define the genre. "Sex, pure and simple, seemed to be the principle ingredient.

Denunciation of 'Massage parlor television' and 'voyeurism' only brought more viewers to the screen...a lot more seemed to be promised than was delivered, but *Charlie's Angels* nevertheless ended its first season as one of the top hits of television. (Brooks, Marsh 114)

Critic Katie Kelly took a more impassioned approach in knocking T & A:

I have, in my mind's eye a kaleidoscope of women who have contributed greatly to our society. Everyone from Eleanor Roosevelt to my Mom. And every time I am forced to look down Chrissie's [Suzanne Somers] blouse or watch yet another string bikini quartet, I can't help but think we are insulting Eleanor Roosevelt. And we're not being that nice to my mom, either. (Kelly 95)

In the midst of this dissent, along came *WKRP*, featuring perhaps one of the sexiest women on TV. Although Anderson brought her intelligence and sophistication to the role, given the climate of jiggle TV, critics found themselves equating Anderson with the other jiggling, giggling females. Unfortunately, this defeated the purpose of Wilson and Anderson's master plan for the character. "I like to trick expectancy," said Wilson. "I don't like to do the predictable. So that was in the plans right from the beginning. I'd get this bombshell blonde that you thought was going to go 'eh,' and actually she had the wisdom of the ages behind her" (Wilson).

Other's felt that there was a different motivation behind Wilson's creation. Some critics charged that Ms. Marlowe was an accommodation that allowed *WKRP* to have the best of both worlds—jiggle and sophistication. "...*WKRP* is going after a broader, somewhat different audience," read one *TV Guide* article.

The rock milieu provides instant identification for younger viewers, of course...but the most egregious accommodation is the casting of a stunningly sexy blonde...compromises have clearly been made; no one ever acted—or looked—like that in the old MTM newsroom at WJM in Minneapolis. [MTM President Grant] Tinker...acknowledges the show "is our attempt to have it both ways—to do our kind of comedy but still get an audience in this new comedy cycle." (Feuer, et. al. 18)

What ultimately became lost in all of this debate was the perception of the positive effect that Jennifer had on television. Unable to see beyond her stunning beauty, the critics missed the birth of a highly significant character. Furthermore, in their haste, they showed us that we are all susceptible to making judgments based on prevailing stereotypes.

During a 1979 interview in *People*, Howard Hesseman advanced an interesting description of Jennifer: "On *WKRP*, [Jennifer] doesn't use sex to get people to do what she wants...Rather, she lets people volunteer to do what she wants because of what they fantasize about her" (Hoover, Reiley 114). This may be the best explanation of the problems the critics were having; it was not what Anderson was doing, but, rather, what the critics fantasized her as doing.

"Pleasantly Stunned by Beer"

Although the commotion over Jennifer was of concern to the press, most of the folks at *WKRP* had little time to pay it any mind; they had a show to do. With five days per week to put together each half-hour episode, the *WKRP* staff quickly settled into a regular working schedule. Waiting for their offices to be readied at KTLA, the writers worked on the first episodes while at offices in CBS Studio City on Radford Avenue in Los Angeles (Chehak).

Ellen Graham, a *Wall Street Journal* writer who spent some time with Wilson, Chehak, Hunter, and Dial, painted a picture of a blue-jeaned writing staff that sipped scotch out of paper cups as they struggled for ideas. Occasionally, as Graham reported, ideas that the writers felt positive about one day would seem to fall flat the next. Hugh Wilson was particularly troubled over what he considered to be a cheap sight gag in "Hoodlum Rock," an early episode in which WKRP promoted a punk rock concert. Toward the end of the script, someone was to sit on a pie. "We've resorted to sitting on pies," moaned Wilson. "The whole damn show's a sight gag" (Graham).

"We should watch these shows like the rest of America does," suggested Dial to Graham. "Pleasantly stunned by beer" (Graham).

A more sober description of the show's writing process was advanced by Chehak: "I can remember we all sat in a room and we pitched general ideas. Then we went off and we wrote very intensive outlines—full rich outlines. Then we'd go and change this and change that. Then we'd get an okay to do things individually and then we'd write the scripts. And in the first episodes, Hugh would always take the final pass on it. More so, he would change Blake and my scripts more because [Blake and I] were more like rookies and Dial was friends with [Hugh]. But he would change [all of the scripts] a lot" (Chehak).

The actors were also an important part of the *WKRP* writing process. "...We'd come in and do a table reading on Monday morning," recalled Richard Sanders. "After that, the actors would start blocking the show. The writers would take what they heard from the table and then go and do re-write...As we developed, we asked to have writers on the [floor] so, as we were rehearsing the scene...changes could be made.

"That wouldn't happen on a lot of other shows, especially during rehearsal, but we would try to keep better communications between the actors and writers, working to improve what we had on the floor. We asked to have a writer on the floor all the time, and then he would take things back and forth..." (Sanders).

The final revised script would be published on Wednesday. Thursday was reserved for blocking and other technical duties. On Friday, *WKRP* shot two shows before a live audience. The first show was done at 4:30 in the afternoon and the second was taped at 7:30 that night. Because they were not getting the reaction they wanted from the earlier audiences, *WKRP* very quickly went to a closed afternoon taping. "Four pm is a strange time to go see anything," commented Sanders, "...so we cut out the live afternoon show. And then we'd do the [later] show for the audience and we'd try to run through the show as fast as we could so the audience could keep fresh in their minds what was happening. A lot of shows will shoot a scene over and over and over again. When you do that...you completely lose the audience. There are times when [any show] will have times between scenes, but we always tried to keep that down to a minimum" (Sanders).

KTLA in Los Angeles

All of the work in that first season was enhanced by the closeness effected by KTLA, which, at the time, was a small (by Hollywood standards), rickety studio with canvas covered, tent-like dressing rooms (Sanders). Being out of the MTM mainstream also helped draw the group closer. "It was a neat group," said Chehak. "The first thirteen shows—you know, the biggest star on there was Howard Hesseman, and he wasn't really a star then. So we had this wonderful honeymoon. A real family situation. I remember after every show...we'd always go out. We'd go out for dinner and drinks or whatever—every show. I think it's rare for that to happen in series TV. I never had it again on any other half-hour. I never had any other half-hour like *WKRP*" (Chehak).

Chehak feels that the first season was further enhanced by the fact that most of the writers were new to series television. "You gotta' remember that we were all just fresh to this," noted Chehak. "And, what was going on at MTM already—they were in their heyday...*Mary Tyler Moore* writers Brooks and Burns were already superstars in writing seven years of shows, and this was Hugh's first show that he pitched—his first show on the air. We were like these wild-eyed kids, you know, just going after it, and, for me, it was like magic. I couldn't believe I was doing it.

"Well, I think the first year reflected that freshness. If anything, the thing about the first year was this enthusiasm and this real freshness that we all brought only because we probably didn't know what we were doing" (Chehak).

Chehak also felt that Wilson served as an inspiration to the writing staff. "I really wanted to do an incredibly wonderful, brilliant job for Hugh—being as fresh as I was, I don't think I did as wonderfully and as brilliantly—but, that was the kind of leader Hugh was—you wanted to do really well for him" (Chehak).

An Improv Feel

Part of the magic of *WKRP* also came from the wealth of contribution that was accepted from everyone on the cast and crew. Wilson, a great fan of improvisational comedy, wanted to foster as much of a repertory atmosphere as network TV would allow (Fong-Torres 17). He was open to everything, including Hesseman's suggestions for Wilson's enlistment of various *Committee* members.

"I think it was the second episode, in other words, the first episode following the pilot, where we used Dick Stahl from *The Committee*," said Hesseman. "...Then, three or four down the line, we used Kathryn Ish, Richard Stahl's wife, from *The Committee*. We used Peter Elbling that year on a show with Michael Des Barres and another British actor—rocker. Peter Elbling was a member of *The Committee*.

"...Hugh was always wide open to suggestions for actors if I knew before hand what was going on with a script. In many instances I would say, 'Gee, you know, there's an actor you really oughta' check out from *The Committee*, his name is...' And [Hugh] would always see them with that kind of handle on their name. [He was] always quite open to suggestions I would make anyway. I mean, I think Hugh had real respect for actors and what they do" (Hesseman).

Wilson even found himself, along with Dial, Chehak, and Hunter, in "Holdup," an early first season episode. Hugh, Tom, and Blake played cops while Bill played station engineer Bucky Dornster. "Yeah, 'Holdup' was a funny show, too...," noted Wilson. "It was when Fever did a remote at an appliance store...I'm the cop who comes in and says 'Hands up,' you know, and all that" (Wilson).

According to Wilson, the Screen Actor's Guild was not too pleased with non-actors working in series television. "We got a letter from the Screen Actor's Guild saying, 'Don't ever do that again.' Which I had thought was really a bit much. I'm taking my life in my own hands letting these actors direct who had never directed before, and letting them write, who had never written before...and then when a couple of writers have two or three lines in the show and SAG comes in and slaps us with a $500 fine" (Wilson).

Indeed, *WKRP* actors did write and direct. This was encouraged by both Wilson and Grant Tinker. "One of the great parts of the first year were Grant Tinker's visits to the set," recalled Jump. "And, I was extremely impressed. I knew of Mr. Tinker and I had a chance to really, I think, get to know and understand him a little better as an actor working for him on *WKRP*. But, here was a man that would come on the set and say, 'What do you want to do as an actor? Do you want to just be an actor, or do you want to write or do you want to direct or produce?'

"And Richard Sanders said, 'Well, I'd like to write.'

"So he said to Richard, 'Then, get at it and submit some of the stuff to Hugh Wilson' " (Jump).

Sanders, who had done some other writing projects with his friend Michael Fairman, took Wilson and Tinker up on their offer. During the first season, the two wrote "A Date with Jennifer" and "A Commercial Break."

"...I had some ideas for the show and I didn't know whether I was going to present them or not," recalled Sanders "...I talked to them about writing a spec script, where Les takes Jennifer out to an award banquet. Les had just won the Silver Sow Award...I just gave that to Hugh one day and Hugh looked it over and he called me before Christmas and he told me that we could do it. That was a lot of fun,...but it also made me very nervous" (Sanders).

One of the funniest scenes from that episode involves Les getting up the courage to defy Carlson's recently instituted policy against employee dating. To the tune of "Hot Blooded," Les donned a sport coat, an ascot, and a recently purchased Mr. Macho toupee. Though Sanders had written the script, that scene was Wilson's invention. "I remember the day that happened like it was yesterday," said Chehak. "I remember we were sitting around and Hugh had been coming in on the freeway and had heard 'Hot Blooded' on the radio and was really excited and was saying, 'We got to get this.' He did that whole thing that Les did on that show—He just acted it all out" (Chehak).

"Commercial Break," dealt with the ethical problems Carlson and Travis faced in selling advertising to a funeral service that functioned like a chain-store. "In that situation, Hugh said that he didn't have a script for next week," said Sanders. "And so Michael and I worked furiously all weekend. We got done with the script and then we showed it to Hugh, and he said, 'Okay, we'll use it.'

"You know, that was great...Hugh was very encouraging. You know, Frank Bonner directed some of the scripts...Tim Reid also wrote some of the shows...and, at various times, Gordon directed and Howard directed...It was really nice to have Hugh allow us to do that—allow us to branch off into other things...Very few shows...allow you to do that.

"...Hugh Wilson set the tone. It was one of those work situations where you'd have people contributing. You would even have the guys who were operating the boom who would shout down lines saying, 'How about this?' " (Sanders).

During the rehearsals for "Turkey's Away," one of *WKRP*'s finest episodes, a boom operator suggested that Hesseman use the Credence Clearwater Revival tune "It Came From Out of the Skies" for the portion of the show after the turkey drop. "...I figured that, well, other than the guys in Credence, there might be two dozen or 1,200 other people that are going to get that," said Hesseman. "Who knows? But, it's fun to do that stuff. I don't think it has to be so broad that everybody and his ancient great grandmother gets the joke" (Hesseman).

The Show that Saved a Life

"Turkey's Away," written by Bill Dial, is one of *WKRP*'s funniest and most famous episodes. Based on a real life incident that occurred at a Texas shopping mall, the show is recalled by cast members with a great deal of pride. In that episode, Jump, who counts the show as one of his favorites, uttered what may be one of TV's most famous lines: "As God as my witness, I thought turkeys could fly" (Dial, *Turkeys Away*).

Jump still gets comments and praise for his work in that episode. "I was at a meeting," said Jump, "and someone said, 'You know, I was talking to someone in a restaurant who is in broadcasting, and he made the statement to me'—this was a woman talking—'he made the statement to me that one of the funniest and most quoted lines in American television broadcast history was, "As God as my witness, I thought turkeys could fly."

"She said, 'He said it in a restaurant—I started laughing. He started laughing. We could not control ourselves—we were laughing physically and out loud over that line in the context in which it was used...People all around were looking at us and then started smiling. And, in some instances, started chuckling, too.'

"It's just one of those marvelous moments that—If you look at that show, the entire show built to that one last line. And, I guess that's one of the reasons why people enjoy it so much" (Jump).

Jump also recalled how "Turkey's Away" once saved a viewer's life. "I was doing a coast-to-coast night time radio gig on ABC," said Jump. "And a trucker got out of his truck and went to the phone booth and he asked to speak to me, so they finally put him through. And he said, 'I have to tell you that you saved—you literally saved—my life.'

"I said, 'How did we do that?'

"And, he said, 'Well, I had just come off the road—I drive a big rig—I had just come in off a long trip. I'd been away for three weeks and I came back and I walked in the apartment and there was a letter on the coffee table and I opened it up. My wife had written a Dear John letter—she was gone, out of the apartment—and it was all over and goodbye.

" 'I dearly loved her and I had never felt such pain and depression. I don't know why I did it, but I went over and I switched on the television and sat.

" 'Then, all of a sudden, this *WKRP in Cincinnati* comes on and it's a show about the turkeys...I must tell you that before the half-hour was over, I was rolling on the floor, laughing. It didn't make any difference any more what was in that letter. I just want to thank you' " (Jump).

"We Played a Lot of Cards"

For all its moments, the first-run of "Turkey's Away" didn't even make it to the air before the series' mid-first season hiatus, which began the second week of November. Though off the air, it was business as usual for the *WKRP* gang. Production and shooting continued as the cast, staff and crew waited for the hiatus to end. Wondering whether they needed to write any scripts beyond the first 13, Chehak recalls that they also played a lot of cards. While things were tense, Chehak claims that he wasn't overly anxious about the show's fate.

"...it wasn't scary because I was so wide-eyed," said Chehak. "Now, when I look back on it all...I realize that it's very rarely that a show goes past 13 episodes. It's real rare if you have a pilot made, but then, if you get off 13, you're really happy to get 13 on the air. Then, if they take it off, you know, you move to the next one.

"After *KRP*, I went on and I did four other half-hour sitcoms and they all didn't make it past 12. The show I'm working on now, [*Alien Nation*]—we just got our back-order for nine, and that was a pleasant surprise.

"You get calloused...you get very used to it. I mean, for me, *WKRP* was the beginning of all the excitement of Hollywood, but it was also the end of my innocence. It was no longer magic. It was work and disappointment and fear and paranoia—all that stuff started" (Chehak).

Howard Hesseman was not particularly apprehensive during the hiatus, either. "I think, speaking for myself, I didn't feel insecure," said

Hesseman. "I felt like the show would probably go back on the air. And, if it didn't—Well, you know, basically, I looked at the whole experience as a string of 'ifs,' you know?

" 'Gee, if I get this role, that will be great. If the pilot actually sells, that will be even better. If it gets on the air, that will be terrific. If the audience really likes it, that will be better yet.'

"But all along I had the feeling that I was doing good work and I enjoyed the character and I enjoyed most of the people, so, at whatever point it all ceased to exist, I would just be sorry that it wasn't going on, but I really don't—I try not to live my actor's life looking at the worst possible future occurrences. I just figured it was good for as long as it lasted" (Hesseman).

During the time it was off the air, CBS received a great deal of mail protesting the show's removal. Hesseman was particularly pleased: "...I think it reflects well on the show that...the bulk of the mail that was coming to CBS was instigated by DJs—by the radio broadcast industry—urging its listeners to complain about the disappearance of the show.

"I know from experience that the show was discussed by a lot of DJs and radio personalities, particularly rock jocks. They would discuss the show the next day. They would talk about it. They had found a means of identifying with it. And, I think, that, in that sense, we had this huge kind of lobby group out there. Disk jockeys, in effect, who went to considerable distance in mobilizing the listening/viewing audience to do something about letting CBS know that they didn't like the fact that we were off the air, and to complain when we were moved so frequently when time went by" (Hesseman).

In later seasons, as the show was moved around the schedule, protests continued to pour in. "Now, that never stopped CBS," said Hesseman, "but, at least they knew that people out there were watching the show. Now, it may have been their considered opinion that obviously these people liked the show and 'they'll find it no matter where we put it.' But that again, to me, speaks to the incredible stupidity on the part of broadcast executives at CBS" (Hesseman).

Jump felt that managers of various CBS affiliates also played a role in getting the show back on the air. "The show was taken off just prior to an affiliate board meeting which was held, I think, in Hawaii," recalled Jump. "...And, some of the people I knew were at the affiliate board meeting and had made the statement that they felt the show was a great show. And, I think that they had brought enough of their feeling and concern to the network executives that they decided to go ahead and give it a second start" (Jump). Chuck Schnable concurs with Jump's observation, saying that *WKRP* was a favorite program among affiliate station managers.

"A Dynamite New Comedy Series"

The new year brought new life to *WKRP*, which returned on January 15, 1979, in the 9:30 Monday night time slot following MASH. The return made history itself, albeit for another network; Ron Hendron, a TV critic on the *Today* show, began following a new NBC policy that allowed its reviewers to plug programming from other networks. Hendron put the policy to the test, recommending the return of *WKRP* over the NBC made-for-TV-movie *Charleston*. Mincing no words, Hendron said that *Charleston* was, "a bad, bad show. But never fear. There is a bright side to Monday night. A dynamite new comedy series, [*WKRP*], is back in a different time slot on CBS" ("Biting the Hand" 64).

Immediately after his review, Tom Brokaw remarked: "For those of you who were wondering whether a critic on this program would ever say anything bad about NBC, there is your very explicit answer" ("Biting the Hand" 64).

Realizing that it had been a while since the show was off the air, the producers decided to do a flashback episode. "It was a recap, where we were explaining the budget to Momma, which was an interesting way of letting the audience be reminded of what had gone before in the series," explained Hunter.

Set behind MASH, the numbers for that and future *WKRP* episodes soared. The bigger audience was rewarded with the distinctive irreverence that made *WKRP* so special. Being part of the industry itself didn't keep *WKRP* from knocking many of broadcasting's conventions, including commercials. During that first year, viewers were introduced to many WKRP clients old and new. Some of those advertisers included Rolling Thunder European Regularity Tonic and Bo-Peep Safety Shoes. Don't forget WKRP's "oldest and dearest account," Shady Hills Rest

Home, whose spot asked the age-old question, "What happens when I can no longer feed myself?"

The new format brought new accounts: Red Wigglers, "The Cadillac of Worms;" Mr. Macho Hairpieces; Heinrich Mauser's World of Oriental Bargains; Weisenheidle Beer—"The beer with the smiling face of Archduke Ferdinand on the label"—and Hutchin's Community Hospital, "Where malpractice is rapidly becoming a thing of the past."

WKRP also introduced America to a number of sleazy characters not normally seen on network TV. There was Randall Ferryman, whose goal was to sell burial plots the way McDonald's sells hamburgers. There was Reverend Little Ed Pembrook, a religious huckster who sold items such as Dead Sea Scroll Steak Knives and John the Baptist Shower Curtains to his Sunday morning followers. Hoodlum rockers "The Scum of the Earth" honored the Queen City with a visit; a take-off on the growing punk rock scene, "Scum" was known for their deplorable demeanor and outlandish lyrics. One "Scum" lyric read:

Love is Murder
Murder is Love
I'm a rock and roll hoodlum
With a black leather glove

Knock me down, baby
Step on my face
I'm a fool for you, baby
Let's blow up this place (Wilson, *Hoolum Rock*)

There was Murray Gressler, the cocaine peddling promotions man from On Slaught records, and Doug Winner, the DJ who eagerly snorted Gressler's payola. There was hyper Del Murdoch, the fast talking owner of Del's Stereo and Sound. A down and out DJ named Bob "Boogie" Burnatt hijacked a live remote at Del's. We also met Arthur Carlson's neo-Nazi prepubescent son—no normal TV kids on this show—and T.J. Watson, Jennifer's old Rock Throw, West Virginia boyfriend, played by singer Hoyt Axten, also visited the station.

Many of the scenes had their own edge of satire, particularly those involving Fever. In one episode, Fever displayed his distaste for top forty by throwing darts at a Barry Manilow "This One's For You" poster. Fever also had a bout with an LSD flashback, another TV sitcom first.

In another episode, "Fish Story," Fever and Venus took part in a drunk driving awareness campaign. While on the air, Fever and Venus were directed to drink alcohol at regular intervals. The State Trooper administering the experiment then tested the DJs' reaction times. While the cop wanted to prove that reaction time goes down significantly with each successive drink, Fever's reactions kept improving.

"Make it Stupider"

Of all the episodes they had done, "Fish Story" became the bane of the series. "The network kept saying, 'Make it funnier, make it funnier'," recalled Wilson. "And I was saying, 'Make it stupider, that's what you guys want—stupider.'

"...Finally I guess to show that I could do stupid as well, I said 'Okay,' and I wrote this show—I think it was the highest rated show we did that year. There was another station, WPIG, and they had a guy in a pig costume going to rock concerts and all of that. So I put Herb Tarlek in a fish costume...cause K-R-P—carp—is a fish, you know...and I did this ridiculous thing where he had to crawl under the toilet—this flapping fish.

"I was so embarrassed by it. If you ever see it, on the credits it says written by Raoul Plager...I invented that pen name...that would be my *nom de plume*...we all decided Raoul Plager...was from Argentina and he had come up and was writing sitcoms and was the son of an SS officer..." (Wilson).

"Raoul Plager wrote a couple of our episodes," joked Bonner. "We didn't mean to hire him and Hugh certainly didn't want him on the staff, but he made his way into the annals of television history anyway.

"Some people saw 'Fish Story' and loved it. We would have fun poking little jokes at other areas. The M.O. of *WKRP*, which we tried to adhere to, was we'd do two or three fun episodes and then hit on a topical subject..." (Bonner).

Even when *WKRP* featured a topical theme, it was done in a different manner from most sitcoms. In "I Want to Keep My Baby," for instance, an unmarried teenage mother leaves her baby to Johnny. TV had been doing the old "baby-in-a-basket" story for years, but *WKRP* added a new twist; rather than reuniting mother and baby at the end of the show, the mother ended up leaving Cincinnati, laying the baby's fate in the hands of Child Services. Again, realism was the key, a quality which *WKRP* would never compromise.

Who Is Gordon Sims?

Perhaps the most meaningful episode from the first season was "Who Is Gordon Sims?" The last episode shot that season, it was actually the first script Chehak had written, back when he was still at his Studio City offices. "I had some idea that it would be neat if Venus Flytrap had some past and came up with the idea that he was a [Vietnam] deserter," said Chehak. "And, of course, we all worked on embellishing that into making the back story..." (Chehak).

Chehak put a lot of research into the script, reading a number of books written about the war. Chehak also talked to a number of Vietnam vets who hung around at a Subway shop across from the Studio City lot. He was looking for a good story to use in the final scene of the script, which served to justify Venus' decision to desert. "There...was one guy, who was working in the Subway," recalled Chehak, "and I'd go over there and I'd say, 'Okay, tell me your worst story today.' And he'd tell me these awful stories. The one I wanted to do we couldn't do—it was too violent" (Chehak).

According to Tim Reid, CBS was not too keen on doing a story about a Vietnam draft deserter, particularly when the deserter was a supporting character on one of its sitcoms. "Hugh submitted this script," recalled Reid, "and they said, 'No, we don't want to do that one.'"

"What happened was production got the best of us and it came down to where we had one more show left and they didn't have a script ready. It would have cost the company a lot of money to delay filming of the last episode because the talent was supposed to get off for hiatus. So, Hugh said, 'Well, I just happen to have one script and I think that it's ready to go.'

"So they looked at it and said, 'Alright, let's do it.' But they had a lot of extras added to it. They had to have a military adviser. So, a person from the military came and sat in on our rehearsals. They were very concerned about it" (Reid).

The network's alleged fears were eventually squelched by the tasteful script, which had Venus turning himself into the Army. "Who is Gordon Sims" spoke to a number of important issues, including the generation and color gaps that existed between Carlson and Venus. It also chronicled some of the horrors that Vietnam vets had been forced to endure. "We did the show and it became a show that was really a turn-around show for the series," noted Reid. "It made a statement. It had interesting and topical information, with a little pathos thrown in, and the viewers loved it" (Reid).

Jump, whose character played a large part in helping Venus resolve the situation, recalls that the show was very well received by the studio audience. "The audiences we had were always very enthusiastic," said Jump. "But the audience that saw that show I think was one of the most sensitive and enthusiastic audiences that we had in the history of *WKRP*. And they were with that show every moment that it was being produced. And, it proved, I think, to be one of the most sensitive and one of the finest shows that we did" (Jump). Home viewers were also pleased with the episode and Reid recalls receiving a number of positive letters from Vietnam veterans.

Reid also received an interesting award for his performance in that episode. "It was an award given to me by the Marine Corps at the half-time of a Marine Corps football game in San Diego. They drove me out in the car and gave me an acting award. Most actors usually get their awards at the Dorothy Chandler Pavilion—in tuxedos...I was out in half-time with leathernecks in football jerseys at a Marine Corps football game and I got this acting award, which I cherished. The whole irony of the thing seemed to fit my career until I received the Image Award for acting in a comedy...and an Emmy nomination for *Frank's Place*, (one of Reid's subsequent series). So, I'm one of the few actors who can say he has an acting award from the Marine Corps" (Reid).

Viewers honored *WKRP* with another award—their loyalty. By the time it went into summer re-runs, *WKRP* became a hit, averaging a phenomenal 38 share, with roughly 16,400,000 viewers tuning in per episode. In a 1979 *TV Guide* interview, Hesseman tried to explain *WKRP*'s phenomenal success. "The show doesn't go for the gags. It goes for identifiable people, a broad range of personalities, all basically good people trying to make something happen. Viewers appreciate that— Following MASH doesn't exactly hurt" (Hano 27). Hesseman would soon find out, however, that time slots were a double-edged sword, and that not following MASH could be devastating.

Chapter Five
"CBS in the Valley"
The Second Season

At the entrance to CBS Studio City's Sound Stage Two is a plaque that reads: "On this stage a company of loving and talented friends produced a television classic. The *Mary Tyler Moore Show* 1970-1977" (Alley, Brown 237). In its second season, *WKRP* set up shop at this historic site (Sanders). The new home seemed appropriate; after all, Hugh and Company were also a group of loving and talented friends.

While some of the players would fondly recall the closeness of KTLA, others welcomed the change. CBS Studio City—affectionately referred to as the MTM Lot—certainly offered more amenities. Gordon Jump, an avid chef, was given a room with a kitchen; in return, Jump agreed to make his famous lasagna for the cast and crew at least once per season. Howard Hesseman, who often referred to the MTM lot as "CBS in the Valley," seemed to enjoy its privacy and comfort.

"It was infinitely more comfortable," said Hesseman. "I mean, not to denigrate the lot we were at the first season, but MTM still had—from the old studio days—standing dressing rooms. I mean, they had adjacent dressing rooms that were real rooms. Two stories of them built on the outside of the sound stage itself. I had a lovely corner dressing room that over-looked where the L.A. river passes by on the edge of that lot...I looked down over the greensmen's area where all the gardens were—where the greensmen keep all the green, growing stuff that they use to decorate sets.

"It was a large room with a couple of couches and a desk and a phone and table and a big wardrobe armoire, and a full bathroom with a huge shower in it. So, when I finished a show I could go up and take off my wardrobe and get in the shower, scrub off my make-up, get all that crap off of me, and get dressed. There was room for six, eight, ten people to sit out in my dressing room while I was doing this. And we

69

could go out and eat—go do something. Much different than most dressing room facilities allow an actor" (Hesseman).

Personal comfort was not the only improvement. Now part of the MTM mainstream, the inhabitants of the "island unto itself" could breath a little easier. "There's a nice thing that happens when you're working on a hit show," observed Blake Hunter. "You're a little more secure...The first year—it was a little nip and tuck there. That happens with all shows, by the way. Unless you're a *Cosby* or a *Roseanne* that starts out to be a huge hit. But, usually it takes a while for the show to catch on" (Hunter).

WKRP had "caught on." In the first part of the second season, still in it's 9:30 time slot, an average of 17,600,000 people were tuning in. The average share for the period between September 17 - December 3, 1979 was 34.2, with no share dipping below the all-important 30 mark.

This success brought attention from a variety of groups, which, not surprisingly, included the recording industry. "We did play some songs as they were coming out," recalled Wilson, "and the record labels, they figured this out pretty quickly. So they're trying to break records all over the place; why not break records on a radio station that 14 million people are watching every week?

"So I got on the mailing list for radio stations...It was great...I got God knows how many free records, and I got all these displays...we put the displays actually in the station, which the legal department went nuts over, because they hate to mention any brand names or actual things, you know. And we started putting these posters up in the station and I became inundated with...sales men were calling on me and...it was kind of fun...

"You should have seen my office. I looked like a point of purchase manufacturer. I'd take them home to the kids and they were thrilled" (Wilson).

Real Issues for Real People

With the realism of the station firmly established, it stood to reason that *WKRP* would involve itself with a number of real world issues; in fact, the list of topics presented during its second season reads more like the index of a news magazine than a catalogue of sitcom episodes. For example, the season opener "For Love or Money" was a two-part episode based on the growing issue of palimony.

Fever was surprised by a visit from his former lover Buffy Denver, a singer who lived with Johnny in L.A. Fever thought that Buffy came back to rekindle their old flame; Buffy, however, felt that Fever stole her chance at a singing career and had returned to get her fair share. When Buffy announced that she intended to sue Johnny for half of what he is worth, all Fever could do was wish her well: "I hope the taxi [you're in] explodes and that the debris scatters for miles and miles" (Magquire).

Much of the comedy for this episode was inspired by the chemistry between Hesseman and former *Committee* member Julie Payne, who played Buffy. "We started rehearsing that show Monday morning," said Hesseman, "and in the afternoon she and I were improvising so much stuff in rehearsal that we got Hugh and a couple of the other writers to come down, and said, 'Look, if we do a little more work and create a few more scenes here, basically we've got a one-hour show or a two-parter, because, I mean, listen to this material—it's really good stuff.'

"And they agreed, and before Monday was over, they got permission from CBS to do that. But that was a gas because Julie and I were accustomed to working together—we had a long standing professional relationship—a friendship—we understood one another's approach to the work, so it was easy to improvise—to write on our feet—to come up with stuff. And that was a joy and we shot all that in one week" (Hesseman).

Abortion was another topic covered. "The Patter of Little Feet" concerned Arthur Carlson's wife's late-in-life pregnancy. One of Jump's favorite episodes, Jump suspects that he and his wife provided the inspiration for the Hunter script.

"My wife and I, at that point in time, were sort of fun, crazy people, you know, and we didn't know that we were being observed as we were coming out of the studio one night," recalled Jump. "We went dancing down the street together. You know, sort of ala Gene Kelly and—*Singin' in the Rain*—and we were just sort of whistling along and swinging our hands and doing little dance steps going down the street.

"Behind us was Blake Hunter, and he was watching what we were doing. And the idea, I think, of middle-aged people having those sort of close relationships—I think it stimulated a thought process in him and it wasn't long before they were telling us about this show they had in mind" (Jump).

The episode was very well received, and, for its sensitivity, was given special mention in a "Close-Up" in *TV Guide*: "Arthur Carlson's wife is pregnant," read the copy.

...Though Carlson is delighted with the news, his...spouse Carmen is fretting. And the Big Guy's joy soon gives way to doubt, with the arrival of overbearing Mama Carlson, who tells her son "...An abortion is possible and legal. You think about that." ("Close-Up" A-64)

Carlson did think about it. On one hand, he wanted the child and was excited to have a second chance at raising one properly; after all, Little Arthur, introduced in last season's "Young Master Carlson," was less than the ideal child. Furthermore, Carlson's strong religious convictions emphasized throughout the series presented a moral conflict with abortion. On the other hand, Arthur did not want to risk Carmen's health. Assured by their doctor that Carmen could handle the stress, the Carlsons decided to have the baby.

Chosen to play Carmen Carlson was Allyn Ann McLerie, who had played the tough-as-nails secretary on *The Tony Randall Show*. A character actress of great breadth, Allyn portrayed Carmen as a soft-spoken, gentle woman who was the direct opposite of the abrasive Momma. She was a perfect complement to Arthur Carlson.

All in the Family

The family atmosphere that Wilson had been after was firmly established by the second season. A number of back stories done since the beginning of the series had shown that station WKRP was staffed by a number of people who were either displaced or somewhat removed from their original families. Fever was a twice divorced loner and wanderer—a 40-year-old who admittedly still lived like a college student. Travis had also been up and down the dial, last hailing from Sante Fe, New Mexico. Venus, as we learned in the first season, was a Vietnam deserter who had been forced to bury his past. Bailey was originally from Chicago, and Jennifer, as noted in the first season episode "I Do, I Do...For Now," had given up all ties to her backwoods, Rock Throw, West Virginia upbringing. Like the rest of them, Les was single and lived alone, although he was still close to his mother who lived in nearby Dayton.

Even the married characters were somewhat at odds with their family life. A number of episodes made it obvious that Herb was dissatisfied with his wife Lucille and his kids Bunny and Little Herb (although he still loved them in his own way). While Carlson was dearly in love with his wife Carmen, his troubled, neo-Nazi son and overbearing mother were often too much for even the kind-hearted Carmen to counter. Thus, finding little connection to their own families, the staff of WKRP often turned to each other for support.

The ingenious method that Wilson used to effect this family atmosphere was wonderfully described in Bill Dial's second season episode "Baby, If You've Ever Wondered." The Arbitron ratings had just been released and the WKRP crew was ecstatic—they had actually picked up some listeners, going from 16th to 14th place in the Cincinnati market. As the rest of the gang congratulated themselves on a job well done, Andy fell into a deep depression; realizing that the format change alone would have accounted for the increased ratings, Andy felt as though he had accomplished nothing in his year at the station. Not comfortable being in a losing situation—Andy had a history of working at high-rated radio stations—he seriously considered leaving WKRP.

Andy felt that the main problem was that his friendship with the staff was destroying his ability to lead; he shared this concern with Venus. When Andy lamented over not firing Herb and Les, Venus brought up an interesting point: You can't fire the little guys without firing the Big Guy—and you can't fire the Big Guy because his mother owns the station. This pivotal observation not only showed the mechanism that Wilson had used to create his fictional family, but it also justified Herb and Les, two characters who, in the real world of radio, would have never survived (Dial, *Baby*).

In a world of television that had been dominated by goofy neighbors, mouthy maids, and silly employees who had no purpose other than comic relief, it was refreshing to find a show that actually provided logic and reason to support the existence of its sillier characters. Even in *The Mary Tyler Moore Show*, we never had a real understanding as to why Ted Baxter was retained, other than the underlying belief that the WJM crew was a family. *WKRP* went beyond this simple emotional reasoning, however, by providing this perfect, Carlson-centered justification. This is not to suggest that Ted Baxter was any less of a character than Les Nessman—Indeed, Ted Baxter still remains one of the finest and funniest characters to date—but it does serve as an interesting tribute to

Wilson's ability to bring credibility to a fictional work.

Credit should also be given to Dial, who brilliantly brought this aspect of the show to life. Unfortunately, this was Dial's last script for *WKRP*. Both he and Chehak left the show to pursue other writing projects.

Sitcom Writing Made Easy

Some of *WKRP's* best episodes were written by Peter Torokvei and Steve Kampmann, who joined the *WKRP* staff in the second season. Like many writers hired by Wilson, neither Peter nor Steven had any previous television experience. "Steve Kampmann and myself came from Second City—the theater in the Toronto Company," recalled Torokvei. "And, we had made a pilot for a TV show idea that we made up in Canada before we came to Los Angeles, which was a dub-in show. We had taken an old episode of *The Cisco Kid* and wiped the soundtrack clean and laid in our own soundtrack. We had arrived in Los Angeles to try and sell this tape and just to find work as actors and writers, just to make our move from the small pond to the big one. Our manager, Bob Manahan, who has since passed away, was the casting director for *WKRP* in the first year. He...took this tape of ours to Hugh Wilson, who was delighted by it and asked us to write an episode for his show.

"We didn't have any other work, so we said, 'Sure, okay—we'll write an episode of a sitcom.'

"We hadn't seen the show before. We didn't know—we worked in the theater—we worked the same time as prime time hours—so we didn't know what was going on. They got us a bunch of tapes and we watched the tapes. It was just a delight. You know, it was pretty unusual for [a sitcom]. We thought we were kind of cutting-edge comedy guys in the Second City Theater—so, the idea of a sitcom—we were already prepared to do a lot of mocking. Well, this show—We thought it was hilarious. There was nothing to mock. The jokes were the best jokes I'd ever seen on television, and some of the best jokes I'd ever heard.

"So, we found a book—we got a book that told us how to write a 30-minute sitcom. We read that and we tried to think, 'What personal payoffs can we get here?'

"We thought, 'Gee, we both really wanted to meet Sparky Anderson.' So we wrote an episode that involved Sparky Anderson....He was fired [from the Cincinnati Reds] while we were writing the episode and he had gotten hired by Detroit" (Torokvei).

Torokvei and Kampmann found Sparky to be a willing guest star who shared a number of stories that enhanced script. "He was just great," observed Torokvei. "Can you imagine just hanging around listening to stories? And a charming, just really nice guy—a truly nice guy. You could see how he could motivate young players. Motivate a team. The show was about the fact that the show that [WKRP] had hired him for wasn't working out and that they had to fire him. So Sparky gets to deliver the line, 'Every time I come into this town I get fired.'

"He tells Art Carlson about the fact that when he has to tell a kid he's cut from the team—that he's no good—the kid thinks he's talking about life when all he's talking about is second base. It was really nice— that came directly from Sparky. He was neat. It was really neat" (Torokvei).

Wilson liked the script and hired Torokvei and Kampmann as story editors, a title that essentially made them staff writers. Steve Marshall and Dan Guntzelman also joined the staff that year. These four, along with Wilson, would become some of the series' most prolific writers.

"Brain Damaged Executives"

Despite the excellent humor and pathos found in the series, the beginning of the end was near. After the tenth episode of the second season, CBS pulled *WKRP* from its Monday 9:30 slot and moved it to 8:00 p.m. That move, along with four other shifts that same year, caused the loss of an average of 2,500,000 viewers. Toward the end of the season, into summer repeats, *WKRP's* shares drifted between the low 20s to low 30s; the day of the high 30 and low 40 shares were over. This was extremely frustrating to those involved with the show.

Hesseman could find no logic in the change. "Going into the fall— going into the new second season, I mean—only a mental pygmy would say, 'Let's not leave them there for another year or so, and build a real following'," complained Hesseman. "I mean, it takes somebody who's— it takes a brain damaged executive—to decide that it would be a good idea to move them. But, that was the decision made regarding our show. Not the first time that had happened. But, I think one of the most disastrous mistakes that CBS made with regard to our show was that decision in the beginning of the fall second season. Because we were doing very nicely behind MASH, and we were starting to pull numbers, as I recall, in that time slot. And, I don't think we were there—the season started in September and I somehow have a memory of moving in November or early December. I mean, it just seems like some kind of suicidal tinged sabotage. It was just nuts!" (Hesseman).

Chuck Schnable, who did not, at that time, make any decisions regarding programming changes, and who is a person held in high regard by Hesseman and many others connected with *WKRP* quickly dismisses the idea of network sabotage: "Well the philosophy always is that a program that seems to be showing strength is needed as soon as possible to shore up other nights and other positions," explained Schnable. "The schedule is the most important thing at the network. So, if they feel that they have a strong property that can shore up another night or another situation, why then, the shows are moved to accomplish that situation. They're selling the nights as a whole package, so it's very necessary to get as much value for each property as possible in that way. If you look at the history of MASH, it was the same kind of situation" (Schnable).

MASH was another show that had great difficulty in finding its audience. When it debuted in 1972, it failed to place in the top 25 shows of the 72-73 season. Interestingly enough, as with *WKRP*, MASH debuted in an 8:00 lead off position, but, unlike *WKRP*, MASH was surrounded by relatively weak competition. When it was moved behind *All in the Family* the following year, MASH placed fourth overall. Though it was moved again the following year, it was positioned behind the successful series *Good Times*. These two moves thus gave MASH two years of strong lead in support and, in 1974, it ranked among the top five shows (Brooks, Marsh 808-10).

Even with that strong two-year boost, MASH's dominant standing was not completely secured. When MASH was moved in 1975 behind the ill-fated *Big Eddie*, which starred Sheldon Leonard and Sheree North, the series dropped to 15th place in the year-end ratings. It took another move and another year for MASH to re-enter the top five. However, in 1975, when it was moved behind the weak hour drama *The Fitzpatricks*, MASH again dropped from the top five, slipping to ninth place overall. It was not until 1978 when MASH was moved to Monday nights that it began scoring consistently well (Brooks, Marsh 755-71).

Obviously, if an award-winning American icon such as MASH had problems finding an audience, surely the network should have expected

WKRP to encounter the same trouble. Perhaps if *WKRP* had been given an extra year behind MASH, it might have fared better, possibly allowing the series to stretch beyond its four season run.

Perhaps it was this realization on the part of those involved with *WKRP* that made it difficult for Schnable to explain what was going on in regards to the network's decision. "Well, from their own personal point of view," said Schnable, "when they had the best slot on the network, following the top show of MASH, and then they were moved to another spot, it wasn't easy [for them] to see another point of view. And I could only try to explain it as best I could and, as it turned out, they weren't always good decisions made by the network management" (Schnable).

"We Can't Do This"

That poor network decision—along with others like it—ultimately meant that fewer viewers were able to enjoy what amounted to some excellent first-run TV, including one episode written by Tim Reid. "Family Affair" was an insightful piece that looked at racism from a different angle—not the overt racism generally equated with red necks and Klan members, but the tacit racism that exists, to some extent, with all of us.

"*KRP* was one of the first shows to really deal [with racism] outside, let's say, of *All in the Family*," noted Reid. "But *All in the Family* did it from a white point of view. You know, showing how racism was dealt with from a white point of view...I mean, how racists have to deal with it and all the emotional changes that they have to go through to deal with their problem.

"But, I wrote a script called "Family Affair" where it dealt with Andy Travis' sister coming to the station. And, because Andy was tied up, he wanted to [have someone] chaperone her for a day. He went around to everybody in the station except me...And it was psychological...He psychologically did not even think of me. So, for the first time, and probably the only time in our four year run, it was really racially—subconsciously—a racial decision not to talk to me.

"It just so happened that time and the way the character of mine worked there, I happened to be the only one who was available, and...I happened to be in the room. Fever couldn't do it and I said, 'Well, I'll do it.' And Fever definitely had no racial consciousness and he said, 'Okay, fine, great.' And we went off, had a great time, and I called in and got someone to fill in for me.

"When I came back, Travis and I got in to it. And we almost got into a fist fight. It came out that it ended in a bar, right near the radio station where we hung out, where we dealt with it openly, you know. We have these racial things deep in us. They're like roots. They're dormant, but they're there and we don't even know it sometimes. And it was really dealt with very openly and very honestly.

"And then a redneck in the bar made a racial comment and I went up to confront this issue. In the script that I wrote, I hit this guy and knocked him out. He made a racial slur—remark about boy or nigger or something like that—and I knocked him out" (Reid).

Apparently, that final scene presented a problem. "Well, when the script went to [the] network," continued Reid, "...they came back [and said,] 'Wait a minute. We can't do this. You can't have a black man knock out this white man on network prime time television. Hugh came back to me and said, 'You gotta do something here' " (Reid).

According to Chuck Schanble, who was responsible to read each script on behalf of the network, making suggestions independent of those handled by Standards and Practices, the eventual change which had Venus and Andy act together in decking the racist was not instigated by the network. "The version of that script that I got was the one you see," said Schnable. "So they must have done their changes in their story meetings between themselves" (Schnable).

Regardless of who had ordered the change, Reid was upset: "I said, 'I'm withdrawing this script if they're not gonna let this happen...we gotta have a payoff.'

"So, the compromise was made that Gary Sandy and I would hit the man at the exact same time. And that's the way that show aired. We got into an argument—who was gonna hit him—and, then we both hit him at the same time and the compromise was made. It was one that I could live with because my character's dignity was salvaged...he acted to protect his own self—he didn't have to have a white character protect his manhood, he could stand up for himself. And it saved the network in the sense of their concern at that time because then it was a mutual thing—it was family against the outside. So [here was an example of] all of those issues that we dealt with way back in 1979; and television was ten years behind the times then" (Reid).

Before shooting "Family Affair," Frank Bonner—who, unlike Herb, lived for adventure—had broken his leg in a parasailing accident. Wilson was forced to incorporate Bonner's accident into the script (Murphy 26). While he may have been upset at Bonner's swashbuckling, Wilson knew that he had good stock in Bonner, who joined the growing list of *WKRP* cast members who entered the production end of the series as a director.

Bonner's first work behind the camera was "The Doctor's Daughter." While some actors find it difficult to direct their peers, Bonner soon found that he was more than equal to the task. The cast's respect for Bonner's ability seemed to help. Whether acting or directing, he had the reputation of being a perfectionist, a label he is not entirely comfortable with. "I am [a perfectionist] with regard to myself. But I have no qualms about actors who I'm working with not being perfectionists. That is, if they want to try different things...I am always open and ready and willing to do that, because I find that the exciting aspect of acting" (Bonner).

A Study in Responsibility

Going into 1980, WKRP was faced with a real-life event it could not ignore. On December 3, 1979, 11 Who fans, aged 15 to 22, lost their lives outside of Cincinnati's Riverfront Coliseum.

The tragedy was slow in building. According to *The New York Times*, people with general admission tickets had been lining up outside the stadium since early that afternoon. An hour before the concert, the crowd extended to the bridge over the Ohio River that links Cincinnati with northern Kentucky (Reginald).

When the Coliseum was late in opening its doors, the fans grew restless. The Who began warming up. Many of the ticket holders feared that the concert had started without them. Anxious, a crowd of fans at one of the banks of doors began breaking windows. The doors flew open and then, "as if propelled by a slingshot," the crowd at that door stampeded inside. In addition to the 11 killed, eight others were injured (Reginald).

While police and fire department officials brought control to the scene, the concert began. No one in the stadium, not even The Who, was aware of what had happened until after the performance. In the aftermath, candles were lighted, laws were passed, editorials were written, and the people of Cincinnati tried to make sense of a senseless shame.

Two thousand miles away, Steve Kampmann was also looking for answers; it was a story he could not ignore. How, in the confines of a sitcom, could a writer find a way to pay tribute to such a tragic loss? "It was a wonderful study in responsibility," said Jump. "First of all, Hugh Wilson felt that it could not be done because we were a comedy show. [Steve Kampmann] said, 'If we were a station in Cincinnati, in order to maintain our license, we would have to deal with that problem. I think that we need to deal with it on our show.'

"Hugh said, 'Well, if you think you can do it, you go ahead and try.'

"...Steve came up with the [original] script and then he went back to his office. All the writers got around him and, of course, all the writers jumped on that thing like a dog on a bone. They finally came up with the episode that you saw and took it to Hugh. And, Hugh said, 'I think, probably, this will work.'

"Hugh took it to the network and the network said, 'You know, if we can put this on the air, every family in America will at least know what festival seating is all about. Up to this point, parents, at least, don't know what we mean when we talk about festival seating—this would be a wonderful way of educating the American people' " (Jump).

According to Bonner, the network's attitude, however, began to change. "When we started rehearsing that episode," recalled Bonner, "the second or third day of the week CBS came down and said, 'No. Uh-uh. We can't do it. We're not doing it. It's too sensitive, find something else.'

"So, Hugh said, 'No—screw you—we're going to do it. In fact, I'm going to go down and make it unanimous. I'll go down and be very democratic about this and ask the actors.' So he came down either Tuesday night or Wednesday morning and said, 'We've been asked to change the show. They're afraid of our treatment of the subject and the possibility exists that they won't air it. What do you think?'

"We said, 'Let's stick with it. We like it, we think it's important, and, after they see it, they may change their minds and say yeah.'

"So we continued. CBS said, 'Well, we'll see it first before we air it. We don't know. We're not giving you thumbs up on this.'

"Then Cincinnati called and said, 'Forget it. We will pre-empt you that night. We won't air the episode if you continue.' They were trying to use scare tactics to get us to deviate from our normal course....We didn't...we finished the episode" (Bonner).

"It was difficult in dealing with the CBS station there," noted Jump, "because they couldn't relate to how we were going to talk about that problem in a situation comedy."

The Cincinnati CBS affiliate, according to Jump, was so vehement in their complaints against the show—a show they hadn't even seen—that they even refused to give the production company news footage of the candle-light ceremony that had taken place the night after the tragedy. Continuing to threaten to pre-empt the show, the Cincinnati affiliate agreed to view a closed-circuit rough-cut of the episode provided by Schnable. After receiving the feed, the Cincinnati affiliate decided to air the show (Schnable).

"Ultimately, they loved it," recalled Bonner. "We got a lot of positive reaction from it. We got some letters from the parents of the victims saying 'Thank you.' CBS, I think, was primarily concerned that we were going to make light of it, being a comedy show—how you would make light of a tragedy that was so fresh at the time is beyond me—but I think that was their reason for their concern. Then they saw it and said, 'Oh. Well, this is kind of a nice episode' " (Bonner).

"In Concert's" significance should not be under-estimated. Following in the tradition of shows such as *All In The Family* and *The Mary Tyler Moore Show*, *WKRP* proved once again that sitcoms can be a viable vehicle for responsible, meaningful messages. What is particularly significant in this case is that, rather than dealing with a general issue in general terms, *WKRP* treated a fresh, specific instance that was laden with reality. One does not see "In Concert" as an exploitation of a tragedy, but rather as an exposition of a problem. It was a struggle to make sense out of a tragedy. In one rare moment, TV tried to help us find a solution.

"We Didn't Mean to Do It, Bert"

Another second season episode also coincided with the headlines, but this time it was quite by accident. In early 1980, Bert Parks, who had become an American institution as host of Miss America, was fired by pageant director Albert Marks. A few weeks later, *WKRP* aired "Herb's Dad," an episode featuring Parks as Herb Tarlek's father. Many people thought that *WKRP* had devised the show in response to Park's ouster. That was not the case.

"We did the episode late December and it was New Years when Bert found out—close after he finished taping the episode—that he had been ousted," said Bonner. "...I recall people thinking that we grabbed him and shot the episode to embellish on the fact that he lost his job, which was not true. It was just one of those things. He came in and did it and it was after the taping that he lost the job" (Bonner).

Ironically, "Herb's Dad" concerned the senior Tarlek's refusal to go into retirement. "It was very spooky," commented Bonner. "It kind of gave you that chill. It's like a prophetic episode. We all just went, 'We didn't mean to do it, Bert.'

"That was a special episode for me," continued Bonner, "because when I was in high school I was always teased by my classmates about looking like Bert Parks. It was just so ironic, you can't believe it. I recalled that for years and years and years. When I got older I used to do a fun parody and start singing, 'There she is, Miss America...' because I always used to get teased about looking like him. Little did I know in my high school days back in the fifties that the gentleman would be playing my dad. It was quite ironic" (Bonner).

Torokvei, who wrote the episode with Steven Kampmann, was delighted with Park's performance. "He was wonderful to have as a guest...On a pure entertainment level, he was interesting to have around. A guy from almost vaudevillian background to have on a TV show is terrific. I remember when we were taping him...And Bert Parks...would turn to the audience the whole time and play all his jokes to the house as though he was on a vaudeville stage. So it was fun just to watch" (Torokvei).

Torokvei also had fun in writing the script, particularly because he always enjoyed writing scripts that dealt with Herb, a character that Torokvei considered to be much more realistic and interesting than, say, Jennifer Marlowe. Torokvei figured that, because Jennifer was such a strong character, exploring her too deeply would force a breakdown in the strength she had built. Herb, on the other hand, was this foible laden fool whose back stories would serve to further define the role (Torokvei).

Bonner agreed that character development was the key to Herb Tarlek's success. "When you create a character who is pretty well labeled 'a jerk,' in order for that character—for that jerkiness—to work, you've got to explore what the man is about," explained Bonner.

"You've got to see him in-depth and kind of get an idea of what makes him tick. If you don't have that—if you just have a brash, arrogant kind of situation where you don't see the other side of these people—then they're not much fun and you don't come to care about them anymore. You go, 'Okay. Great. He got his. Good. Get him off the show.'

"It's important when you're playing a heavy or someone who is on the other side of social amenities, you've got to give him something where people can have fun with him. What's important to me is when I go on personal appearances and people come up to me at these different cities or in the airport and they say 'You know, I just love to hate you.' Then you know that it worked" (Bonner).

The final scene in "Herb's Dad" was particularly touching. Herb, who obviously loved and idolized his father, could not bring himself to touch the man. This created an interesting tension between the two. "We talked about [touching]," recalled Bonner. "'Do we do this or do we not, you know—what do we do?'

"And then Bert and I kind of talked about it and I thought, 'No, we're a couple of, in our own minds, Macho guys.' And we said, 'Let's don't. It puts too much of a period on it. It gives you no place to go after that.'

"Like on *Moonlighting*, when Bruce Willis and Sybil Sheppard finally slept together. Now what? The same thing on *Cheers*, with Dansen and Long [after they slept together]. Even though I'm a fan of *Cheers*, with that kind of thing, you go, 'Well, okay—Now what?' So, we opted not to touch there" (Bonner).

Instead, Herb used an interesting piece of business with his pinkie ring to replace the touch. "I'll tell you—some of Herb's characteristics came from a used car salesman I knew years ago who sold me a Mustang," said Bonner. "...And, I remember, when I was shopping around for a car, I noticed that he wore this ring—I think he wore a college ring—it was kind of big—And I'd note that whenever he was in doubt about a question I'd ask him about a car, or when he had to think for a moment what was the right answer, he always kind of twirled that ring on his finger or went to it. I just recalled that so, when I found myself a nice piece of costume jewelry, I said I'd try to remember this little thing and use it" (Bonner).

"Herb's Dad" illustrated an interesting difference between *WKRP* and run-of-the-mill sitcoms like *Family Ties* or *Different Strokes*. While the latter programs are filled with characters who wear their hearts on their sleeves—name one *Family Ties* episode that does not end with the words "I love you"—*WKRP* shied away from this sort of cheap, easy emotionalism. When Herb Tarlek, Sr. tells his son that he loves him, the audience hopes that Herb will verbally respond; the fact that Herb does not provides a lode of emotion that could not have been mined had Herb given in. It is much like the *All in the Family* episode in which Mike and Gloria left for California. The audience wanted Archie to say, "I love you, Mike," but Archie, who would have been out of character in dealing with that emotion, couldn't. It is the principle of less-is-more, a concept that *WKRP* had down to an art.

Chapter Six
A Study in Reality
The Third Season

In the summer of 1980, The Screen Actors Guild initiated a strike against theatrical and prime time producers. Effectively shutting down film and television production, SAG demanded higher wages for its members and a resolution to the problems concerning actor's compensation for industry profits generated by pay TV, videodisk and video cassette technologies (Tusher 1). As the strike continued into early fall, the resulting production delays wrecked havoc with network prime time schedules (Knight 51). The lengthy strike postponed most first-run programming until mid-October.

As the strike neared a conclusion, Richard Sanders and Michael Fairman began putting together a new script for *WKRP*. Many radio stations had been sponsoring marathons; Sanders and Fairman felt this could make for a very colorful episode, particularly if the entire cast shot it on location in Cincinnati. With the strike still in progress, however, SAG would not allow the entire cast to work. Getting a special waiver, Sanders and Fairman went to Cincinnati to shoot scenes for a modified version of their script, "The Airplane Show," which featured Les Nessman flying around in a rickety old plane piloted by a disgruntled veteran played by Fairman.

The stunt flyer hired to play Fairman during the aerial scenes was found at Ohio's King's Island amusement park. Sanders was to have a stunt double, as well, but a problem at the last minute forced Sanders to go up in the plane himself. "The stunt double got sick," recalled Sanders. "So they shot it from a helicopter and I was up there in the plane. I don't know what the heck got into me to do that, but I was in the plane doing stupid stunts like that. I was halfway out on the plane's fuselage...there was no way in the world I could have survived if I would have fallen out. The plane was a 1934 Wacco—you had to be careful—if you stepped off, you'd step through the wing" (Sanders).

This was not the first time Sanders had gone to Cincinnati on business for the show. "We would go back there and do parades...they had people there who were selling T-shirts that said *'WKRP in Cincinnati'*," said Sanders. "I think the people in Cincinnati, in general, really liked the show" (Sanders).

Sanders, who was often invited to speak at various agricultural events and, of course, hog contests, traveled to other parts of the country, as well. Identified so strongly with his confused news character, he would often appear at these functions as Les Nessman. "It was much more fun that way," admitted Sanders.

Dance of the Mental Pygmies

Many of *WKRP*'s other actors would also do promotional appearances for the show, including Howard Hesseman who, during *WKRP*'s four-year run, spoke on a number of radio stations across the country. On an episode of *Saturday Night Live*, Hesseman and Harry Shearer did a sketch based on some of the actor's experiences with various radio DJs. "That was all real stuff [in that sketch]," recalled Hesseman "...I mean, some of [the DJs] were quite decent—some of them were real mental pygmies, too.

"I remember going to a San Francisco radio station one day, sitting down—it was like on a Thanksgiving week, or a holiday or something—sitting down with the guy and he hit the pot—he was off the air—and, as the music was playing, he said, 'Okay, here's a list of ad-libs that I put together from one of these radio services that I subscribe to. It's some pretty good jokes. You know? Like, if you could say this then I'll say that. Or, here's a reverse, and you'll say this and I'll say that.'

"I'd say, 'What the fuck are you talking about, man?'

"And he said, 'Well, you know, this is like stuff we can do.'

"And I said, 'Why don't we just talk? Why don't you ask me whatever you want to ask me? Or say whatever you want to say? And I'll ask you what I want to ask you and I'll say what I want to say. And that's what will pass for conversation in between the records.'

" 'Well, I just thought some of this stuff was kind of good.'

"And, I'd say, 'Gee, I don't know. I think you got the wrong guy—I didn't come in here to do a scripted show with you. I thought I was coming because you wanted to interview me and you wanted to have me on the air with you in your show. That's what I'm prepared to do. But I'm sorry, I'm not prepared to read these jokes. So, what do you want to do? I see your record is getting close to over. I see your engineer [waving]...'

"So he'd say, 'Okay, I guess we can try to talk.'

"He was one of those guys who—It's true for most people working in radio and I suppose rightfully so, but it's really maddening,—was just terrified of dead air. So, he would ask a question and if I hesitated in the slightest while perhaps considering my answer, he was babbling.

"So, the first time we got to another break and he's got some music going, I'm saying, 'Look, man. You asked me a real question. At least, it passes for real over the air. I'm giving you my answer. Please give me the courtesy of allowing me to deliver the answer at my own speed. I'm not completely oblivious to the fact that we're on radio out here. I'm not gonna' get up and go into the other room and look up a word in a thesaurus as an answer for you. But, I'm trying to respond in an honest and human fashion, and not like a machine and not like a show-biz personality. And that's the deal. If we're gonna' talk, we're gonna' talk. We're not gonna' do a miniature radio version of John Davidson's TV talk show where he says, "Well, we got three minutes left, tell me all about yourself." God, there's enough of that shit in life.'

"Well, those kinds of situations were always interesting to be in. It was seeing how far any of those guys—they weren't all men; some of them were women—were willing to take the chance. To ride the gain, as it were, and see where it took us.

"...So, that's what that was like for four years. It was incredible idiots and some really gracious, warm people who I could deal with. [Some of them] were connected to their community, they really did love their job, dug the music, and appreciated the work of all the other people around them who contributed to what they were doing. In those instances, it was terrific to be there, although I must note that I usually had to emulate Fever and do the morning drive time show, from 6-10. That was never real great" (Hesseman).

Torokvei's Finest (Half) Hour

Early in the third season, Peter Torokvei wrote "Real Families," one of *WKRP*'s most inventive episodes. Beginning with a cold opening, the show featured Peter Marshall and Daphne Maxwell as hosts of a show that investigated "real families"—in this case, the Herb Tarlek clan. While it looked much like the popular reality programming of the period, the impetus for the episode was Torokvei's disgust with *60 Minutes*.

"I was angry at *60 Minutes*," said Torokvei. "It bothered me that *60 Minutes* was being touted as this brilliant news show. I kept saying, 'As long as it's edited film, it's an entertainment show. It's not news. As much as you act like it's news—or, as much as they package it like it's news—it's not. They're in control.'

"And, really it all started out with sitting around and having a couple of scotches in Hugh Wilson's office one night and talking about...If Mike Wallace phoned and asked if he could do an interview, would you let him come in? I mean, you know he's going to nail you on something. Even if you've led this guiltless life. You know he's going to dig something up, even if it's [only that] you've been rude to your mother...He's gonna' kill you. So, it was that sort of stomping around—sort of ranting and raving about Mike Wallace and *60 Minutes*. And, I was probably jealous, too, of the ratings they got" (Torokvei).

Torokvei's anger toward *60 Minutes* made for some great commentary on TV journalism. The basic theme of the show was that people will do anything—"anything"—to get on TV, a phenomenon upon which TV news relies. Good foreshadowing of conflict was accomplished in the episode's open when Peter and Daphne reported that last week's focus on a Florida dentist and his family had led to the good doctor's arrest. It seems that "Real Families" had found some vials of a controlled substance in the dentist's garage. Thus, viewers had to ask the question: If a respected member of the professional community couldn't stand up to close scrutiny, what hope was there for sleazy Herb Tarlek?

As expected, "Real Families" proceeded to make Herb appear as a fool and a liar. However, toward the end of the show, the real message was made; fed up with the invasion of his family's privacy, Herb evicted Peter, Daphne and the film crew from his house. "Now this is real!" exclaimed Peter (Torokvei, *Real Families*).

Not amused, Herb began to explain that nothing on TV is real, not even the news. This verbal assault provided excellent closure to Torokvei's original theme.

"I'm really proud of ["Real Families"]. That was a gift from Hugh

Wilson. In fact, [for] the three years that I was on the show, he let me play quite a bit with the half-hour format, which got us in a little trouble. Got him in a little trouble every once-in-a-while" (Torokvei, Interview).

Torokvei's unique treatment of "Real Families" did end up causing some problems. "It's one of my favorite episodes that no one saw," said Frank Bonner. "And, the reason being that we were moved around in our time slot quite a bit. People saw this unusual beginning—this cold opening—called "Real Families," hosted by Peter Marshall and Daphne Maxwell, and they thought it was a new show. And they turned it off. It was really interesting. You try to do something a little different and people go, 'Oh my God, Ethel, *WKRP*'s not on.'

" 'Well, let's watch *Bowling for Dollars.*'

" 'Okay.'

"A lot of people who did look at it didn't understand it," continued Bonner. "In fact, I remember a comment made to my mother in Arkansas—I'll show you the intellect that is running rampant out there in Middle America, which is quite scary—[Some woman] said, 'What did your son do last night? What did he do? Take his video out in the back yard and just kind of video tape his family? What was that?'

"They didn't get it. Didn't get it" (Bonner).

Tim Reid, who convinced his friend Peter Marshall to do the show, recalled that Marshall took some flack for the program, as well. "The night after that show," said Reid, "...Peter called me and said, 'My mother called me last night after the show aired and she said, "Peter, I never get in your business, but I tell you, I don't think you should be doing that show".' She thought that that was a real show. She was so incensed that we had gone and exposed sort of the dark side—the mundane side—of human life" (Reid).

Much of the different look for this show came from its singular production. It was filmed with a wide-angle fish-eye lens, and fourth walls were installed on the set to provide a more realistic appearance (Bonner). This technical aspect was enhanced by the improv-like creative discussions that took place between Torokvei and the *WKRP* cast, making it one of the series' most collaborative efforts. "I loved that episode," noted Bonner, "because so much of it was built upon improvisation. When Peter Torokvei...wrote that episode, he'd just kind of give me the situation and say, 'Here's what the deal is. Here's what we want to get out of this scene. Here are the points we want to make. So, let's look at it and see what you come up with.'

"...A lot of it—It wasn't so much improvised on the set as it was when [Torokvei] and I would get together. Probably a week or so before we taped that episode, we'd get together whenever we had a break and he'd say, 'Okay, here's the deal. The guys come in the bedroom there, and they're a day early—you expect them Monday and here it is Sunday morning; what do you say? Here's some ideas I have.' So, it was that kind of thing" (Bonner).

A unique TV event, "Real Families" was reminiscent of some of the inventive episodes done by MASH. Even though many viewers tuned it out, "Real Families" was critically well received. A critic for the *Village Voice* said that the episode restored his faith in television. Torokvei felt that "Real Families" was the pinnacle of his sitcom writing career. "I should have stopped making half-hour shows after that show," commented Torokvei.

Fortunately, Torokvei stuck with it. "Daydreams," another inventive episode by Torokvei, featured each of the characters in fantasy vignettes. As Carlson rehearsed a speech about radio, Venus dreamed that he was a stand-up comic, Fever imagined himself as a rock star, and Andy saw himself as the head of a organized crime family running WKRP. Another fantasy, invariably cut in the syndicated version of the show, featured Bailey as the first woman President of the United States. In that scene, Johnny, America's first "first-husband," and Bailey lie in the same bed that was used by Scarlet O'Hara in *Gone with the Wind* (Torokvei).

Ferreting Out the Dopers

The third season also saw the birth of Arthur and Carmen Carlson's baby. Blake Hunter, who had written last season's "The Patter of Little Feet," struggled to come up with a new and inventive way to show the birth of a child on TV. "We couldn't find anything that was fresh," said Hunter. "And Hugh was wonderful for looking for fresh new ways of expressing himself. We couldn't find anything, so what we ended up doing was sort of very realistic. Allyn Ann McLerie, who played Mrs. Carlson, did a very realistic thing...I mean, the camera was on her as she was supposedly having the baby. There was a hospital show that had just been canceled—a soap, or something—so, we got to use their set. We went into a hospital, and we went up and down the halls and visited other people in other rooms, and it was kind of fun—I enjoyed that. It was different. We didn't do it with an audience" (Hunter).

The episode is filled with a number of comical gems, including a paging system that kept asking the doctors to call their stock brokers. More humor was found in the confusing maze of colored lines that ran along the hospital floor. Trying to find the rest of the gang that had assembled at the hospital, Fever got lost and ended up spending the evening with an elderly woman named Peggy Sue. In an interesting piece of business, Fever, lying down to talk with Peggy Sue, instinctively grabbed for the mask that hung over the hospital bed. Obviously, Fever was hoping that the mask was connected to the gas jet.

"Quite privately—I didn't even share this with Hugh—I just figured that Fever was the kind of a person who basically welcomed any and all opportunities to somehow introduce foreign substances into his body," said Hesseman. "It was just a habit.

"...I just felt that Fever was not carried away by it—not ruled by it—but that he never ruled it out as an option in a situation, either. And, in many instances, it had nothing to do with discussing anything with the writers. I would just decide for myself what kind of condition I was in to do a scene. It was just something to play. It was just something to do as an actor. In some instances, the network itself would say, 'No, he can't do that. He can't be doing that'."

Seeing how many of these drug references he could get away with became sort of a game with Hesseman. "That was one way to ferret out the dopers amongst the network staff," said Hesseman, "because [the dopers] would know—it was great.

"The Standards and Practices person for the last couple of years was...right on it all the time, and we used to have these incredible moral dialogues, where I was saying, 'So, you're probably going to smoke a roach on the way back to your office, right?'

" 'Well, yes, I am.'

" 'So, how do you feel about doing your job,' I would reply, 'when it entails saying things like you've said to me today [against Fever's drug references in the show]?'

" 'Well, that's a completely different thing.'

" 'Well, I don't understand how it's a different thing. I mean, if you're telling me that I can't, in any way, appear to condone what you call "anti-social behavior," and, yet, you, yourself, in your private life, are pursuing, by your own corporate definition, anti-social behavior, what do you—are you Catholic? What do you talk about with your priest? I'm curious. I'm not talking to you as an actor...it's just Howard Hesseman and I'm talking to you'—whatever her name was—'one on one, sort of like doper to doper. Do you get my drift? Well, how do you feel about this?'

"[She'd say,] 'Well, it's the network's position...'

" 'No, no, no, no, no,' " I said, frustrated with her not understanding my point.

"And every year at the wrap party she would say, 'You know, it's really fascinating talking to you about these things all season, and I hope we can continue to work together and I hope next year will be even more fruitful.'

"So, I'm saying, 'So, are you gonna' offer me a hit of some really good shit outside now, or are you just going to leave it with this kind of corporate gratitude? I mean, what are we talking about here?'

" 'Well, Howard, you know what I mean' (Hesseman).

"That was great fun. But that's all behind me now." Indeed, Hesseman has taken a 180-degree turn on his attitude toward drugs. While he is not the type to jump on the "Just Say No" campaign, Hesseman has eliminated all artificial stimulants from his life, including cigarettes, which he smoked for 33 years (Hesseman).

"The Joy of Learning"

One of the most meaningful message episodes from the third season was "Venus and the Man," also known as "Venus Teaches the Atom." Asked by the station cleaning lady to help convince her son Arnold to stay in high school, Venus ended up giving the young tough a very interesting lesson on both the atom and the importance of an education. "That was an episode that Hugh Wilson wrote," said Reid. "It came out of a situation where his wife was studying medicine—studying to be a doctor at USC. And she was home doing some homework and she had her books [out] and Hugh was just bored and he picked up [one of her books]. He couldn't understand anything in that book.

"And he [asked her], 'Well, look, is this like if you try to break it down to something very simple it makes sense?' [He went and did what

I ended up doing, explaining the atom, with his wife.] It became very funny, but that's the way he understood it.

"Well, then he looked at *KRP* and said, 'Which character could do what I just did?'

"To give you an idea of the kind of mind that Hugh had, he called me and said, 'Look, I got an idea.' He said, 'What happens if we can deal with the delinquency problem with black youths,' which had been and still is a major problem within the community. He said 'We can get something in on this and here's a neat way to do it. And not only that— we can teach somebody something.'

"When he told me the premise, I said, 'Great.'

He said, 'Tim, I'm putting you...I want you to stay on this and make sure that what we're trying to do is accomplished.'

"Hugh wrote the script," continued Reid. "We made very few changes in the script. My job was, of course to do the material, but also to make sure that the initial point that we were trying to make was made. It was an episode that was very difficult to do, but, when it came out, you knew it was special. And that show won him the Humanities award and that show was covered in the high school *Scholastic* magazine around the nation. They did the whole thing—the whole show—in cartoon form. And it was used in study groups for high schools with kids all across the country. Copies were sent all across the country at that time. So that show was very, very powerful because it dealt with an issue in a very positive way" (Reid).

Again proving itself different from the average TV show, "Venus and the Man" did not pretend to offer any miracle cures or false hopes. This was particularly evident in the final scene in which the cleaning lady returned to thank Venus for convincing Arnold to return to school. Asked if he thought whether Arnold would stay in school to finish out the year, Venus admitted that the odds were stacked against her son (Wilson, *Venus*).

This realism helped to enhance the message of the show. Reid feels that "Venus and the Man," presented in the manner it was, also served as an excellent lesson for educators. "We introduced what I think that the educational system should be introducing—the joy of learning. Not that there's a goal where you're gonna' learn so you can get a $20,000 job at the end of the rainbow—it's the joy of learning. And you're usually very old when you discover that. But to teach that to young people early on—

it makes the rest of their life much better. So that episode was very, very powerful, and potentially effective in terms of changing what television does.

"...Television affects millions and millions of people. If you're going to do that, it would be wise, as much as possible, to send some positive information to viewers. And that's what infuriates me about this town— that, all too often, I would say 80 percent of the time—very little thought is given to the message that is being sent out there. And we are affecting negative information. We're setting bad examples for the rest of the masses.

"You see, television is such a potent force. I don't care how many people argue that it isn't—It is *the* most powerful man-made force on this planet!" (Reid).

WKRP's subtle approach to affecting positive information was found in a number of other episodes, including "Out to Lunch," a Torokvei episode concerning Herb's growing problem with alcoholism. On the verge of landing a big account, Herb began growing more and more reliant on alcohol to close his sales. When the big sale he was working on fell apart, Herb, with the help of Carlson, began to face his problem. "Rather than really heavily preaching—rather than using a hammer-over-the-head type message—we kind of let it play in its comedy," explained Torokvei. "Even in that sort of obligatory, serious wrapping-up scene, we still tried to avoid any direct-line preaching" (Torokvei).

Indeed, where other sitcoms dealing with this topic have resolved the problem by having the character pick up the phone (presumably to call the nearest AA chapter) and say "I'm an alcoholic," Torokvei purposely avoided this sort of melodrama. Realizing that it would be pretentious to think that a sitcom could do anything to solve such a complex problem, "Out to Lunch" primarily served as an episode devoted to character development. If it brought up the problem in a viewer's mind, that was fine, but Torokvie's main goal in all of this was to explore yet another side of Herb Tarlek. By maintaining a realistic attitude toward the episode's ultimate affect, Torokvei was able to avoid the pretensions that many other sitcoms often fall prey to when dealing with similar issues.

"They Owed Us"

One issue that presented a perfect target for *WKRP* was censorship. In the early 1980s, Reverend Jerry Falwell's Moral Majority began gathering a great deal of support in their efforts to censor prime time television programs that they felt were offensive.[3] Coming out with special "hit lists," Falwell called upon his supporters to take part in economic boycotts aimed at the advertisers of targeted programs.

"...Those bastards—they put us on their list," recalled Wilson. "...a show that had too much sex and too much violence. So I wrote this guy—Reverend 'Jerk-off' down in Mississippi or wherever...See, I'm from the south and I grew up knowing these guys were bad cats because before the issue was abortion and all it was 'Catholics' and 'Niggers,' you know? I mean, they've always got something—The most anti-Christian group I've ever run into.

"Anyhow, they were very powerful at the time and they put us on this list, so I wrote this guy, this Moral Majority guy, and I said, 'I'd like to know why I'm on this list?'

"He didn't write back. I called him a couple of times with no reply, so I said, 'To hell with it. I'm going to do a show about it. But I'm not going to make it—I'm not just gonna' create a straw dog and burn him down. I'm going to research this and listen to him and let him state the argument. But, then, definitely in the end, show why they're dangerous' " (Wilson).

Upset as he was, Wilson remained true to his promise and presented the facts in a manner that made the writer appear more like a concerned citizen than a personal victim of Falwell. Part of his research included a talk with Gordon Jump, a man known for his own deep religious convictions.

"Hugh asked me..., 'How do you feel about censorship?' " recalled Jump.

"And, my comment to him was, 'I don't believe in censorship.'

"And he said, 'Well, what do you believe?'

"And I said, 'If you teach people correct principles, they can govern themselves.'

"He said, 'That's an interesting concept.' He went back and wrote the show based on that philosophy. He sent it to me and said, 'Read it and see if it offends you in any way.'

"I read the show, and it didn't—I thought it was well done. And it worked.

"What the show did, in effect, was present both sides of an issue in such a way that, after you had seen it, you had to make your own decision as a viewer," continued Jump. "I think it did that clearly. I think we demonstrated that there are definitely two sides to this issue. How far in either direction do you want to go?

"And, the show never had a resolve...because the show didn't rest with us—it rests in the minds and the attitudes of the American people. What a neat thing that—in American television—you can deliver that issue and give the people both sides of that" (Jump).

Jump's general acceptance of the rock format surrounding *WKRP* serves as an interesting comparison of the philosophies found among devoutly religious people. While those like Falwell feel that they have to attack what they consider improper, Jump realizes that there is room for different ideas. That was, in essence, what "Clean Up Radio Broadcasting" was all about.

"[Music] was never an issue for me," admitted Jump. "I love music—any kind of music. I think any kind of music is a form of statement of a culture or a group—a society. I think music is a wonderful way of expressing emotional feelings, whether they are good, whether they are traumatic, whether they are sensual—music has a way of transporting a message. I think that when we turn our backs on messages, we turn our backs on possible solutions to problems that exist within a society" (Jump).

According to a number of people connected with *WKRP*, CBS wasn't all to keen on doing this episode. Indeed, Reid feels that shows like "Clean Up Radio Everywhere" and other politically motivated episodes were part of the reason for *WKRP*'s ultimate cancellation (Jump). However, CBS didn't try to stop the program.

"They didn't like it, but they didn't say we couldn't [do shows like these,]" said Wilson. "They never said no. They were sorry that I was doing it, but they never said no. I think the reason for that was two-fold...one was that it was unpleasant to deal with me...well, I was argumentative, I was pretty single-minded about where I thought *WKRP* ought to be going...

"It's the producers who put the thing on the air...that are good fighters...and it's no fun to have a meeting with a fighter.

"Also, I think there was a slight feeling of they almost kind of owed us, because they had given us so many bad time slots and moved us around so much. I could always go there and say, 'Hey, don't tell me about the God damned scripts; what about these time slots?' " (Wilson).

"Clean Up Radio Everywhere" was one of those stand-out episodes that spotlighted Wilson's ability to deal with issues and transform them into entertainment. "Like any artist," explained Hesseman, "you can try to create stuff that you think will meet the market's demands successfully or satisfactorily, or you can try to express yourself through your art. And, I think that Hugh Wilson, much to his credit, certainly tends toward the latter a sufficient number of times to make me really respect his work—I have enormous admiration for him as a writer. I was frequently remiss in expressing it at the time. I recognize that. But, I see it now" (Hesseman).

The episode not only allowed Wilson to express himself through his art, but also showed Wilson's uncanny knack for tackling the right issue at the right time. Indeed, the week after the episode aired, *TV Guide* ran an article on the various religious groups that were using economic boycotts to effect a change in TV programming.[4]

Interestingly enough, while shows like "Clean Up Radio Everywhere," "Venus and the Man," and others like them had an air of immediacy during their first-run, they are still timely and fresh today. Censorship is still an issue, and, thanks to the countless number of narrow-minded groups in our society, it always will be. The problem of high school drop-outs will be with us for a long time, as well. While "Herb's Dad" was interesting in its time because it featured Bert Parks, its message on how we treat the elderly is just as important today. Even "In Concert" has a timeless appeal that goes beyond its specific case, for it was primarily a show about what happens when we chose to remain ignorant about the world around us, particularly the world that involves our sons and daughters. Furthermore, Hugh and Company brought us these types of shows without the pretensions or the ego that afflict many of the issue-oriented episodes of other sitcoms. Perhaps this is why *WKRP* has remained so successful in syndication. Unfortunately, any success that it had attained in first-run was quickly on the way out.

Chapter Seven
"I'm Exhausted"
The Fourth Season

There was an interesting irony in *WKRP*'s fourth and final season. On the one hand, WKRP, the radio station, began doing very well. Under an economic boycott instigated by the "Clean Up Radio" people, WKRP went commercial free and began picking up good numbers, eventually "becoming" the number 6 station in the Cincinnati market (Guntzelman). When Andy was able to keep the employees from forming a union, he was rewarded by Momma with more money for the station, which soon received a brand new lobby (Hunter, "The Union").

Meanwhile, *WKRP*, the TV show, was having its worst season ever. While the season opener helped CBS to win its premier week Monday night, *WKRP*'s other first-run episodes that season failed to register in the top 20. "...It was just clear that the show wasn't going anywhere," admitted Wilson. "Because we had 18 time slots, I think, in four years, and I must say that, by the time the fourth year rolled around, my mood was just, 'Cancel it. I'm tired of this. I'm exhausted' " (Wilson).

Frustrated as Wilson was, it did not affect the show's quality; that fourth season included some of *WKRP*'s most inventive, provocative and humorous episodes. "Fire," which featured Herb and Jennifer trapped in an elevator of the burning Flem building, was one of the few TV shows shot in real-time. "To Err is Human" had Herb wind up on a black hair-care product stand-up display that was supposed to feature Venus Flytrap. Herb later ended up making things worse by offending the client, who turned out to be blind. In "Three Days of the Condo," Johnny Fever came upon a financial windfall and bought a condo at "Gone with the Wind Estates." When he ended up hating the place, Fever eventually got out of the deal by pretending that he and Venus were homosexual lovers.

Herb got the thrill of his life in "Changes" when Jennifer agreed to go out with him on a mercy date. Nervously sitting in a restaurant booth with Jennifer, Herb accidentally spilled wine onto his lap. In what was to be his proudest moment, Herb ended up walking out of the restaurant with Jennifer on his arm and a wet wine stain on the front of his pants. On the other hand, Les Nessman found luck in love when he was matched with his perfect mate in "I'll Take Romance." Things went along pretty well until Les found out that the service was merely a front for prostitution.

WKRP also maintained its forthright posture in dealing with timely issues. "Love, Exciting and New" had Andy as the victim of Momma Carlson's sexual harassment. Radio station programming services came under fire in "The Consultant," in which an old friend of Andy's threatened to give the station a bad report unless Andy subscribed to the consultant's service. Proud that he worked at one of the few stations that still programmed its own music—and wanting to hold on to that honor—Andy came up with a funny scheme to discredit his old friend.

"The Consultant" was not the first WKRP episode that focused on the dwindling state of pre-programmed playlists and computer-operated radio stations. In the second season episode "Venus Rising," Venus was asked to become the PD at WREQ, an automated radio station run by a computer affectionately called MAXX.

"What do I do around here?" asked Venus.

"Not much!" replied the station manager, who went on to tell Venus how proud WREQ was of its affirmative action program.

Telling the manager to "Paint MAXX brown," Venus returned to WKRP (Marshall, Guntzelman).

The episode "Rumors" asked the question, "Can male and female co-workers live together and still be friends?" With his apartment being fumigated, Johnny took up quarters with Bailey. Rumors of sexual activity between Bailey and Fever began to fill the station. Even the level-headed Andy and Venus were not immune to spreading the off-color gossip.

"Dear Liar," which had Bailey embellishing the facts of a local news story, was based on an actual scandal that had taken place at the Washington Post. Another headline topic involved over-the-counter diet pills. Forced to air commercial spots they had sold to a vendor of "legal speed," WKRP was faced with the legal and ethical questions associated with advertising such items. "Jennifer and Johnny's Charity" investigated the problems of the homeless, specifically looking at how the rich deal with—or, rather, refuse to deal with—the recipients of their generosity.

On the lighter side of the news, Richard Sanders and Michael Fairman's "The Impossible Dream," had Les interested in going to New York to audition for the CBS Evening News. Still a funny episode today, it was particularly interesting in its original broadcast because, at the time, Walter Cronkite was ending his tenure as the network's most trusted anchor. Who better to take his place than Les Nessman?

Like "The Airplane Show," the episode turned out differently than Sanders had planned. "That evolved because I wanted to do a show—I had talked to Walter Cronkite about doing a show with us," said Sanders. "He had already done something on *The Mary Tyler Moore Show*. There was some interest expressed by Walter Cronkite in doing [*WKRP*], but it was finally turned down because...he was retiring at the time. He finally turned it down...[because if he did the show]...right away, that would have been the first thing he had been in since retirement and...CBS didn't want him to be set up as a news commentator becoming an actor or him going into entertainment—they wanted to keep him doing news. So, instead of Walter Cronkite coming to *WKRP*, we had Les trying to become Walter Cronkite" (Sanders).

"These Guys Really Want to Dance"

Though Les never made it to New York, Venus did spend some time in prison. "Circumstantial Evidence," written by Tim Reid and Peter Torokvei, was a unique episode that showed how blacks can often become the innocent victims of questionable eyewitness testimony. Based on an actual case in which a black man from Texas was sentenced to life in prison for a crime that he did not commit, the episode exposed the deadly serious side of the old "they all look alike" stereotype.

"I wrote this script based on what could happen to any of us if we were set up or had been used. That had been written initially to be a two half-hour episode...but the network at the last minute refused to give us the extra time so we ended up shortening it to a half-hour. So, a lot was crammed in and the ending didn't suit me" (Reid).

In the episode, a beautiful woman framed Venus for a jewelry store robbery. Waiting for his hearing, Venus was detained in the county jail.

Though the episode had many serious undertones, the pathos was froth with humor. "We made some real funny jokes about it...I remember telling Johnny Fever when he first came to visit me, I said, 'I want out of here. I've only been here an hour now and three guys have asked me to dance.'

"I said, 'Really, these guys really want to dance, you know what I mean? You get me out of here now, because either I'm gonna be one hell of a boxer or one hell of a dancer.'

"Now, everybody's doing those kind of jokes, so that isn't that impressive, but we were doing that back in 1981 so, again, the show, as far as I'm concerned, was a trend setter in many ways. The writing was superb" (Reid).

Once the trial was held, the judge found sufficient evidence to hold Venus over for trial. As Venus was being taken back to his cell, another black man, booked on suspicion of robbery, was brought into the elevator. When the accompanying police detectives saw the two black men together, they realized the mistake they had made. This resolution came about as an answer to Venus's silent prayer. While it was a bit miraculous, the resolution showed the spiritual side of Venus that was based, in part, on Reid's own beliefs.

"[Hugh] allowed me a lot of input into what Venus would think about the shows that he did and how he dealt with certain issues. I was going through a lot of personal change in my own life, becoming, I think for the first time in my life, an adult. I was grown up but I wasn't an adult. And I think I was going through changes, seeking things spiritually and emotionally...—Hugh knew that, because we hung out a lot together, and he would put a lot of what I was going through—the books I was reading, whatever philosophy I was into that week—into the scripts.

"A lot of times you'll notice Venus was always the character that was saying to everybody to 'be calm, to study themselves, to center themselves, to breathe deeply'—all those...metaphysical kinds of things my character would get mixed up in. And it came out a lot from my personal life. I was at that time the balancing and centering aspect of that show. The actors—we had a good relationship—and a lot of times they would come to me and we would chat about what was going on in their lives. The character Venus both on screen and off screen...had become sort of a 'soulish' kind of guy.

"It was really a centering kind of character—I would say toward the middle of the show my character suddenly became the center dot and a lot of shows and a lot of stories would come into the center and out. And I would be woven into the plot with a different point of view, which, again, was a first" (Reid).

Reid is proud of the work he was able to do to advance the image of black characters on TV, particularly on *WKRP*. At the same time, he is bothered by the fact that his efforts often went unnoticed. "Prior to that, you have to remember, most black characters in television were very broad," said Reid. "...If there is anything that I sort of regret about the Venus character it's that, in the past, when everybody was doing 'What's wrong in television with black characters' and taking shots, nobody really paid any attention to what was being done with that character and, in many cases, not seeing the positive sides of Venus" (Reid).

"The Creation of Venus," written by Blake Hunter, brought the character full circle. In a very inventive manner, Hunter explored what Venus had been doing before his appearance in the pilot. "What I did was I kept a record, just on my own, of every fact we learned about every character," said writer Hunter. "If in one episode we said that Carlson drove a Dodge, I wrote that into the little book under 'Carlson.' So, in case you were ever sitting in the room and you said, 'Wait a minute—what kind of car did he drive?' You'd flip it to the page under Carlson and it says, 'Well, it's already been established with our viewers that he drives a Dodge,' So, I kept that kind of record. It was just something I wanted to do for the fun of it.

"Under Tim Reid, I had the most incredible mish-mash—he had been a school teacher, he had deserted from the Army—I can't remember all the different things that I had under Tim Reid—but it didn't seem like the whole character. So Hugh let me do a story in which I explained how all of these characteristics came together in this one man" (Hunter).

Hunter got the idea for "The Creation of Venus" after seeing the British play "The Norman Conquest," an interesting trilogy performed in a three-night sequence. On the first night, all of the action in "The Norman Conquest" took place in the living room. On the next night, it would take place in the dining room. The third night, the action would take place in another room. Each play had the same characters, and, if on the first night, one character would walk out of the living room and into the dining room at 9:30, on the next night the character would enter the dining room at that same time. "[The Playwright] had created this little piece of clockwork ingenuity and it was fascinating to me.

"What I tired to do was I tried to re-do the pilot, telling what went on in the other rooms. I didn't do it nearly as well as 'The Norman Conquest' did, but that was my premise. Venus only comes in during the last couple of minutes in the pilot. So, what I wanted to know was what Venus was doing all this time when he wasn't in the room?" (Hunter). As it turned out we discovered that the self-confident, jive-talking Venus portrayed in the pilot was actually a shy, part-time DJ who was very nervous about his first shot at a full-time radio gig.

The Phone Cops

"The Creation of Venus" was directed by Gordon Jump, his first directing job for the series. Although he did an excellent job handling a complex script, Jump tries to downplay his contribution to the episode. "Directors in television really become movers of people—they become traffic cops. Particularly after a show has been on the air for a while. You really just need to be able to give ideas—what I call "thought processes"—share ideas or thoughts with the actors to get from them a fullness—a richness—of what a speech or an idea within the show may carry. Directors also have to worry about all their shots—their camera shots—and the movement—the choreography—of all these people throughout the set—what we call blocking. And basically, that's what the director does.

"Particularly after a show's been on the air—I didn't have to tell these people how to develop their characters. Their characters were already set" (Jump).

Hesseman also got a chance to direct one of the fourth season episodes; "You Can't Go Home Again," featured Arthur Carlson returning to his old alma mater, Otterbine College, which, incidentally, was a school that Jump had attended. Hesseman, who hasn't seen any of the last season's episodes in years, did an excellent job as director, although he wasn't entirely comfortable with the role. "I think it's always weird when you step out of a company in which you work as an actor and direct your fellow actors," said Hesseman.

One fourth season moment Hesseman particularly recalls occurred in the two-part episode "An Explosive Affair." Station WKRP had received a bomb threat from a fanatic group known as "Black Monday." After the building was cleared by the bomb squad, Fever and Venus went to the transmitter on the outskirts of town to continue broadcasting. Out at the transmitter, Fever became frustrated when he was unable to place a bet with his Oriental bookie. When his hunch bet horse "Fever's Break" ended up winning the race, an angry Fever destroyed the phone. Hearing sirens—the bomb squad was on its way because it had been discovered that the bomb was placed at the transmitter—Fever's conspiracy theories got the best of him and he feared that the phone cops were after him. This throw-away line actually ending up drawing quite a bit of attention. "Frequently, people tell me that they really enjoyed Fever's finally speaking aloud on national TV about the 'Phone Police,' noted Hesseman. "Yeah. Great. I'm glad they remembered it. That was just a running gag among me and any number of friends, and many people unknown to me [,as well], but, I sort of thought that almost anybody knew about the 'Phone Police.' There were a lot of people out there that proved my point. They were really tickled to have it out. I mean, it was really funny" (Hesseman).

The "Phone Cops" line was just one example of the counter-culture derived humor that was often present in *WKRP*. This style of humor, provide in large part by Johnny Fever, contributed to *WKRP*'s overall hip and honest appearance. Though usually able to get away with such irreverent commentary, Hesseman felt that there were aspects to his character that could or should have been different. "There were definitely those moments," admitted Hesseman. "It doesn't come to me as the portrayal of the character, it's just that there were specific things that I was asked to do or asked not to do that rankled me a little bit from time to time. I can certainly see with hindsight that, if I was unwilling to see what was so evident at the time, it wasn't only Hugh's wishes. You know, sometimes it was pressure that was coming at him from the network. In retrospect, I think he probably went to battle on my behalf far more often than I gave him credit for.

"The character could not be what I would have really liked for him to have been. But, it is naive for me to think that he really could have been, unless there were major changes taking place not simply in the way television is done in America, but in the way in which people look at what is done on television, and the way America thinks about itself and what life is. There's just a whole realm of human behavior that doesn't exist on television that we all know about. Somehow it's not deemed includable" (Hesseman).

Though a few more seasons and a little more luck may have allowed *WKRP* to effect a few changes in television, that was not to be. Faced with slumping ratings and, according to some sources, what may have been political struggles within the network, *WKRP*'s days were numbered. Though each of the cast members was suspicious of the impending doom, there was still some hope that the series might come back for a fifth year. However, on Wednesday, April 4, 1982, the final first-run *WKRP* episode was aired. It was canceled a month later ("CBS Takes..." 452), and everyone began speculating as to why.

"Maybe You and Me Were Never Meant to Be..."

On the surface, the reason for *WKRP*'s cancellation was simple. "It got bad ratings," says Wilson. "That's what cancels them all" (Wilson). However, a bigger question remains: Why did *WKRP* do so poorly in first-run, especially since it has done so well in syndication? There are many possible answers to that question but, because network television and TV viewing habits are so complex, it is impossible to pinpoint one specific reason for *WKRP*'s failure. Looking at the possible answers, however, provides some interesting insight into the factors that influence television programming.

One explanation for *WKRP*'s lackluster performance may simply be that not enough people found *WKRP* to be a show worth watching. This is not to imply that *WKRP* was a bad show; indeed, the previous chapters have emphasized the talent, creativity, quality and value found in *WKRP*. However, quality and success do not always go hand-in-hand. In a problem that is as old as the medium itself, viewers and critics have often found themselves frustrated by the fact that seemingly mindless shows often have more staying power than shows considered to be worthwhile. Although this is a rather subjective observation, discriminating viewers, TV critics, and media historians seem to be able to differentiate with little dissension between quality and run-of-the-mill programming. Thus, for every ten *Happy Days* or *Different Strokes*-type programs that survive, there is one exceptional, quality show like *The Odd Couple* or *Frank's Place*—or *WKRP*—that, through no fault of its own, fails to score.

If we accept that *WKRP* constituted quality TV—that it was a show worth watching—does this mean that American viewers are incapable of appreciating quality programs? That question, while advanced by a number of TV critics, may be unfair, if only because critical acclaim and viewer response have occasionally been in sync. Perhaps it is better to suggest that there are specific periods during which viewers choose to reject quality TV. Many who study television feel that the nation's political climate or mood may influence the type of shows viewers watch. These people, usually network executives, argue that, when times are bad, people will forsake reality-based or politically involved programs and demand more escapist, mindless or fantastic entertainment. If, on the other hand, the general public takes a more active interest in certain issues, they demand that those interests be echoed in their entertainment (Gitlin 9).

Examples from various periods in recent TV history lend some credence to reinforce this theory. In the 1970s, when the issues of race and sexual discrimination were on the public's mind, shows like *All in the Family*, *Maude*, and *The Mary Tyler Moore Show* survived. This is particularly interesting in the case of *The Mary Tyler Moore Show*, which survived in spite of the fact that it was never as big a hit as *All in the Family*. As a racist and sexist backlash began to appear in the late seventies—spearheaded, perhaps, by the rise of the religious right and, later, Reagan conservatism—people no longer cared to discuss these issues, let alone see them as part of their TV drama or comedy. On the surface, this sort of argument may appear to explain why *WKRP* failed to capture first-run success, particularly during its last two seasons, which coincided with the advent of Reagan conservatism. However, it does not explain why *WKRP* was so successful in syndication, especially since its re-run heyday occurred during those same conservative times.

Thus, we see that there is a problem in trying to relate popular culture to popular moods, particularly where television is concerned. While it is often assumed that culture is dependent upon the moods and attitudes of the public—and, to a great extent, this is true—it is also true that television often distorts realities and fails to incorporate various issues and ideas that are displayed in other forms of expression, such as film and literature.

Consider the fifties and sixties; while sexuality was being discussed in film, it was still common to see married television couples sleeping in separate beds. Not only was this true of Lucy and Ricky in *I Love Lucy*, but also of Rob and Laura Petrie in the otherwise hip and sophisticated *Dick Van Dyke Show*. Also, while films of the sixties saw a growing awareness of blacks and civil rights, TV shows rarely featured blacks until the early seventies. Therefore, if television has a history of ignoring events and values found in the real world, can it be considered a true indicator of our own values?

Hesseman, drawing on nearly 30 years experience in television, feels that programming is determined by more than just a simple reading of popular mood. "Basically, prime time television offers us a highly unrealistic view of ourselves," noted Hesseman. "What it does do is use contemporary events—it uses social problems and attitudes and fads of the time—to hook us into believing, hopefully, enough about ourselves or, at least, what we think is ourselves there on TV. That we'll buy all that other stuff that they're selling us in the commercials so that our lives really will be as sanitized and successful as the lives of the people ostensibly we're watching on TV.

"...You know, it's not an original bitch, man. Most of what's on prime time in American television is fodder between commercials. It's an advertising medium. It's a sales medium. Hugh Wilson was quoted that first season as saying, 'If you ran a bar mitzvah film in our time slot and it got big numbers, it would be a series within five weeks. It would be on the air every Monday.'

"I don't think that the people who are paying what they are paying for advertising time give a damn what the show is. If it's paying off for them in terms of revenue, it comes back as a result of advertising" (Hesseman).

However, if advertising revenue is the bottom line of a TV program's success, and if that revenue is determined by the number of people who buy specific products advertised on various shows, does that not place the ultimate success or failure of a show back into the hands of the American people? Reid doesn't think so. "Well, now, first, you can't say the American people," cautioned Reid. "American people get blamed for so many things just like Jesus gets blamed for everything that happened...The American people are not the ones that determine what goes on television. I know that the fallacy is that they are, but they aren't. The people who determine what goes on television are called the

Nielsons. They're 4,000 strong. It was 2,000 [in 1988, but now] they're 4,000 strong.

"Those people determine what goes on television. Now, of those 4,000, you have to aim your material to suit that demographic. That demographic is not a true demographic of America. I think you'd find of that 4,000, I doubt seriously if 20 [or even] 12 percent of that 4,000 are black. I doubt [whether] the percentages to that this country breaks down regionally are represented in that sampling. I just don't believe it. As a matter of fact, I know it isn't so. However, as a producer and a creator, you have to gear your material for that market. That is the marketplace that you have the advertisers and special interests and all of those things. So, you're not really writing television for the masses, you're writing television for this fictitious—this '2.19' family in America—That's what you're writing television for" (Reid).

Thus, we begin to see that the success or failure of a show, independent of the intrinsic value that show may or may not possess, is the result of a complex, perhaps unexplainable, mixture of network perceptions and possibly stilted sample markets. How, then, can media historians and students of popular culture attempt to explain such a complex situation with simple theories that assume that television is an entirely democratic measuring system of American popular moods and values? The situation becomes further complicated when we begin to realize that there are a number of factors beyond the public's knowledge or outside of the public's control that affect a TV programs success.

This is particularly important in regard to *WKRP*. Reid maintains that *WKRP* was moved about and canceled because the information that *WKRP* tried to effect went against the grain of those in television's corporate structure. "We just offended some people and we had to pay," says Reid. "Same thing with *Frank's Place*. We had to pay...this business of television is very profitable and very powerful. And, like in any business of that nature, one must be careful as to the kinds of information, the kind of going against the power structure—you just have to be careful. It's just part of the business. You take that on when you take this business. And I think that people who come into it with very lofty ways of how they want to do it are disillusioned quite quickly" (Reid).

Frank Bonner speculated that the reason for *WKRP*'s cancellation was a political conflict between CBS and MTM. "Rumor has it that there was a lot of politics involved in the situation," said Bonner, "and that's why we were moved around as often as we were. I guess the production company and the network came to loggerheads—for whatever reason—and the network said, 'Hey, if you don't straighten up and do what we say, we're going to move you. We're gonna kill your show and we can kill it by moving you around'."[5]

Looking at the constant schedule changes, Torokvei also conceded that there may have been some politics involved. "Yeah, it did have a lot [of time slot changes]," said Torokvei. "I know. It was like a network trying to kill a show. They were very silly...Sometimes, you know, I had paranoid times where I thought that—where they just didn't like it...I had those feelings about MTM as well. That it wasn't their kind of show. In fact, that was definitely the vibe on our lot. At the time, *Hill Street Blues* was just starting up and so it was, of course, the tiffany show—and they had a couple of other things around...like *White Shadow* and shows like that. Sort of caring, concerned, classy-looking shows on film. And we were a kind of a raw, taped, cheap comedy. We were sort of like the bad fraternity on campus. There was definitely that vibe around, so maybe the network felt kind of the same way. I don't know. I never really let it concern me, except in paranoid moments" (Torokvei).

Yet another possible reason explaining *WKRP*'s demise was offered by Hesseman, who speculated that *WKRP* may have been victim of a power struggle within CBS. "...I think there were people within the corporate structure of CBS who did not look upon the show as one of their projects, and, thus, were not favorably inclined to treat it with concern—to do it any favors. They were going to do a lot better if a show that they were championing started to do well, or got a good slot and, thus, started to do well. I think also that *KRP* was something of a 'Maverick outfit,' if you like, even within the MTM structure—within the structure of the MTM family. I think the fact that we were off the lot that first year gave us a little more room—a little more latitude to goof around. We weren't being looked in upon as closely or as frequently by MTM's people.

"...I have no real reason to think any of this, except I can look at what happened and how many times we were moved in a four year period—many times in the face of growing popularity, where it seemed like, from some aberrated mind's point of view, [that] we were in real danger of locking into a position in the top 20 for several consecutive weeks. That always seemed to signal a schedule change for us. I mean, it was sort of a joke. 'God, we seem to really be drawing an audience—they found us again. We're really getting popular—the network will no doubt be moving us shortly.' And, sure enough, they would" (Hesseman).

Hesseman's explanation is possibly the most accurate. Indeed, author Todd Gitlin, in his book *Inside Prime Time*, noted that a network often feels that it is better off in canceling rather than saving a marginal show. The reasoning behind that, according to Gitlin, is that it may be easier to sell a new, untested product than one that has a history of poor results.

Still, in fairness to CBS, many of the time slot shifts, as ridiculous or ill-intentioned as they appeared, may have been an honest attempt on the part of the network to find an appropriate audience for *WKRP* aside from the one it had found when it followed MASH. Chuck Schnable, who was not with CBS at the time of *WKRP*'s cancellation, is quick to point out that while networks may make bad decision, it is only in their best interest to see that a show succeeds. Indeed, the idea of a network trying to kill one of its own shows is laughable to Schanble, who, though recently retired, has spent a great deal of time in network programming. If a particular, verifiable incident or series of incidents did serve to bring the wrath of CBS upon *WKRP*, it has remained hidden throughout this scrutiny and most likely will remain so.

No one can say with certainty why *WKRP* failed to become a sustained hit, but perhaps it was because of a combination of the number of factors discussed. One factor was *WKRP*'s inability to obtain a first-run audience, which was most likely because of a combination of frequent schedule changes and strong competition. The possibility of the desire for less involved, less intelligent programming, either on the part of the viewers or on the part of the network, may have also served to limit the audience. Add to this the possibility of there being, at worst, various network animosities toward the show, and, at best, people in the network championing projects other than *WKRP*, and one gets a sense of the sort of uphill battle *WKRP* faced.

"I've Lost a Family"

As sort of a final irony to its last season, after *WKRP* was canceled, nine of its episodes received a 30 or higher share in summer repeats. This may have been due to weak competition. On the other hand, viewers, realizing that the episodes would be edited for time in syndication, may have wanted to get one last look at the full-length shows. If the latter is true, then it is a bit unfair, for while the viewers had the opportunity to bid their farewell to the show, none of the cast, staff or crew had the chance to formally assemble to say their last goodbyes.

There must have been a suspicion on the part of the cast, however, that "To Err is Human" was going to be their last show, for the actors made a special gesture during the episode's Thursday rehearsal that is recalled fondly by Hunter. "As a little gesture of respect for the show," said Hunter, "all the actors—all the men—wore tuxedos on the last Thursday, and the ladies wore evening dresses. So, we didn't know we were going to be canceled, but we also didn't know if we were going to be back.

"There was a great camaraderie on the show—there really was. I've never known actors to do anything as nice as that. I still have pictures of all the actors in their tuxedos and evening dresses on that last show—just a nice little gesture, and I liked that a lot" (Hunter).

After the taping of "To Err is Human," a funny show which, incidentally, was not broadcast during the regular season, the actors went off on hiatus, waiting for the network to decide *WKRP*'s fate. "...The last statement out of the one of the network executives as we were going out the doors was, 'Well, we'll see you...in June'," recalled Jump.

A short while later, the cancellation was announced. Jump was particularly saddened. Although he says that it would not have made him feel any better had he known during the regular season that the show was ending, Jump still has a vivid recollection of the sense of loss that he felt.

"It was about [May] when Hugh called me on the phone, I think, and he said, 'It's all over—there's no more *WKRP*—the network's canceled the show.'

"I said, 'You know, Hugh, aside from the money and the ability to go to work everyday as an actor, the great tragedy of all of this is that eight people who genuinely love each other are no longer going to be able to bring to life the most magnificently written words of comedy that have been coming forth from the writers of the show that I think will make American television history. I really am sad because I've lost a family" (Jump).

Indeed, the family that Hugh and Company had worked so hard to assemble those four years before was now gone—disbanded. Never again would those talented actors and writers assemble together on MTM's stage two. More than that, it would be a long time before another show would come along to provide that same irreverent, biting-the-hand-that-feeds sort of comedy that was the hallmark of *WKRP*. While a few shows of the late 1980s had their flings with breaking the fourth wall and exposing the seedier and seamier sides of broadcasting,[6] none of them accomplished it with the same grace, wit, or style of *WKRP*.

Television is a funny thing. Often as ridiculous and incredible as the programs themselves, the medium is full of surprises. Twelve years after its cancellation, *WKRP* had one more surprise left.

Chapter Eight
"Whatever Became of Me..."
Epilogue

During an interview in early 1990, Gordon Jump said that he felt *WKRP* could have gone on happily for another six years. If he will settle for another four, he has himself a deal; in March 1990, MTM announced that it would produce four more years of *WKRP* for first-run syndication (Mahoney 1). In September, 1991, the new *WKRP in Cincinnati* debuted, with Jump, Frank Bonner and Richard Sanders recreating their roles amidst a cast of all new zanies. Since its debut, Howard Hesseman, Loni Anderson, and Tim Reid have each made guest appearances. Bill Dial, first season writer of the original series, serves as Executive Producer.

The return of *WKRP* was spearheaded by MTM president Kevin Tannehill, who counts himself as a fan of "classic" *WKRP*. Tannehill believed that the original's success would help bolster the new series, which has a budget of around $400,000 per episode, much higher than the usual $250,000 to $300,000 allotted for other syndicated programs (Mahoney 56). In late 1990, MTM repurchased the original 90 episodes from Victory Television, the syndication service that had been distributing *WKRP* since 1982, and now offers both old and new episodes as a package to local affiliates and independent stations (Mahoney 56).

Series revivals, because they are inevitably compared to the originals, are often on shaky ground. History has found that most series remakes have not fared well, either critically or commercially. For each success, there are a dozen failures. For example, while Paramount's *Star Trek: The Next Generation* has done fairly well—even *Star Trek* fanatics admit to liking the new series—*The New Leave it to Beaver* was an abject failure appreciated by only the most ardent *Beaver* fans. Many of the one-shot sequels such as *Return to Mayberry* or *Return to Green Acres* have also been equally disappointing. The reprise of *Green Acres* was particularly troubling to those who found the original series to be one of TV's most inventive and funny comedies. The same was true of *Return to Mayberry*, which left *Andy Griffith Show* fans sorry they made the trip. It goes without saying that any *Brady Bunch* reincarnation has been strictly a "check-your-brain-at-the-door" affair.

Nevertheless, original *WKRP* fans still held out hope that the new series would maintain a legacy of quality. With its first season completed, those fans must surely be disappointed; indeed, while the new *WKRP* is a better-than-average first-run syndication effort—it is even a better-than-average sitcom—it still pales in comparison to the original.

There are many problems with the new series, and, if it is true that the executive producer determines the tone of the show, it is very likely that most of problems can be traced to Bill Dial and his production staff. Dial may have been the one who wrote the classic "Turkey's Away" episode, but now almost every episode he produces is simply a turkey. Rather than integrate the new characters with the old, Dial has held Carlson, Nessman and Tarlek in suspended animation, making for a very lopsided program that is self-glorifying, character heavy, and, in all frankness, plot deficient. It is as if Dial is living off his one hit-episode past, with the first three episodes constantly reminding the viewers of the day *WKRP* bombed a Cincinnati shopping mall with live turkeys. Are viewers expected to believe that this story has been on everyone's mind for the last 12 years to the point that it constantly resurfaces in the daily workplace conversation? It would seem more logical and more rewarding to give viewers new adventures that do not rely on the memory of old series triumphs.

Where the old *WKRP* was froth with reality, the new *WKRP* is mired in standard TV-land fantasy. For example, one episode pits *WKRP* in a city-wide poker match against arch-rival WPIG. The biggest problem with this episode is that it actually expects the viewer to believe that WKRP is broadcasting this poker match as a live, on-air event. In reality, no radio station concerned with dead-air would ever broadcast such a boring, colorless event. However, having an announcer was an easy way to advance the plot; as is so frequently the case, the new *WKRP* compromised reality and good scripting. Indeed, the only thing the new *WKRP* does in regards to reality is outfit its new on-air crew with headphones. If Dial and his crew started caring as much about substance as they do cosmetics, the new series may have a chance.

The above episode has another problem. In a clumsy effort to give some back story to the character Mona Loveland, the sexy new night time DJ played by Tawny Kitaen (who is more reminiscent of *Happy Day's* Pinkie Tuscadaro than Jennifer Marlowe), we are told that Mona is a compulsive gambler. However, this character fault is revealed much too early in the series—and much too callously in the episode—for viewers to care. Furthermore, Mona is supposed to be a strong, sensitive character in the tradition of Jennifer Marlowe and Venus Flytrap. If we recall what Peter Torokvei said about the problems of writing pathos for strong characters, we see that this episode did nothing but opt for cheap emotion while robbing the character of her later potential for strength. And, as a result, the entire episode robbed the viewer of something much more important—the ability to laugh at a well written script.

Such problems appear in almost every episode. Indeed, watching the new *WKRP* is like a schizophrenic experience. For a few moments the viewer can sit there and truly enjoy the series, and then, in the next moment, an extremely stupid moment emerges and makes the viewer feel bad for even caring.

What makes this even more frustrating is that the new series is loaded with talented actors. Jump, Sanders, and Bonner do an excellent job in reprising their roles—they are seldom stock or phony. While Howard Hesseman appeared to emote a bit too much in the first episode in which he reprised America's favorite DJ, his later efforts in the series have proven quite rewarding. Tim Reid's return as a successful broadcasting executive made for the first season's best episode. The only returning character who has been disappointing has been Loni Anderson, who, as Jennifer Marlowe, has become a glorified institution that is hard to accept as a real character—but the problem in Anderson's case lies in the script, not the portrayal.

Many of the new cast members are equally as talented as the veterans. Mykelti Williamson as program director Donovan Aderhold gives a solid performance that never succumbs to the unbelievable zaniness of the other characters. Lightfield Lewis as Arthur Carlson Jr. is also perfect in the role of the character you love-to-hate. Most impressive is how Lewis accomplishes this without mimicking Bonner's character; each are a special brand of weasel (Lewis has since been dropped from the cast).

Even the problems with Mona Loveland are hard to blame on Tawny Kitaen; Given some character direction and three-dimensional dialogue, Kitaen displays a great potential for excellence. With all this good talent in front of the cameras, it appears that the new *WKRP* enforces the lesson brought home by the original series—there must be personnel dedicated to quality behind the camera, as well. With a top-notch company of actors, one must return to the assumption that the new series falls short in script rather than in execution.

But the series is still young. Furthermore, critical viewers will note that the new series has tended to improve with the passage of time. If Dial and his crew can stop reliving the first-season past and improve the scripts, the new *WKRP* may yet prove to be more than just 90 additional episodes that weight down a classic.

"I wasn't interested in being a DJ"

Since 1982, *WKRP*'s cast and creative talent have been keeping themselves quite busy. Howard Hesseman, able to successfully overcome the jinx often associated with playing an extremely identifiable character, has enjoyed the greatest success. Indeed, while other actors such as Dick Van Dyke and Alan Alda have become typecast because of the roles that brought them fame, Hesseman quickly shed his disheveled DJ image and, as quickly as late 1982, began popping up in other situation comedy roles. "The toughest thing was to get people to understand that I wasn't really anxious to play DJs," said Hesseman. "You can't believe the number of DJ roles I was offered in movies and Movies of The Week. [I also received offers] like syndicated radio deals and stuff like that.

"[I had to say,] 'This isn't what I am—I'm an actor. I'm not this guy. I'm not a disk jockey. I'm not a radio personality. I have a nice voice— Thank you very much—but, no thanks' " (Hesseman).

In 1982, Hesseman landed the role of Ann Romano's husband in *One Day at a Time* (Blocks, Marsh 461). From there, Hesseman appeared as Doc in NBC's 1984 live presentation of Mister Roberts, which starred Robert Hays, Charles Durning, and Marilu Henner. In 1985, Hesseman won the starring role in ABC's *Head of the Class*. Playing teacher Charlie Moore, Hesseman provided a few lessons in history and many lessons in life to a group of academically advanced high school students. While the series was very popular and the role did have its moments, neither the show nor the part approached the quality of *WKRP*. Hesseman left *Head of the Class* in 1990 in order to pursue other creative avenues.

Tim Reid has also enjoyed a great deal of success since leaving *WKRP*. Unlike Hesseman, Reid's first work after the series included a stint in syndicated radio. "...That lasted for about two months," said Reid. "...It was too innovative for black radio and a bunch of gentlemen around the country formed a conspiracy and took me off the air. But it was very successful at college campuses. It was a countdown show with comedy. We had cold openings, we did theme shows,—you know, a tribute to Bob Marley—we did all kinds of things. Within that, we would also do the top 20. It was a funny show" (Reid).

After the radio gig, Reid formed his own production company and began working on a number of small projects. Reid also wrote some dramatic scripts for the detective series *Simon and Simon*, in which he also played the recurring role of Downtown Brown. "I think *Simon and Simon* was a quality show for the genre which it was doing," commented Reid. "It was well written and well produced. I was there four years. Of one-hour shows, I think that's one of the better one-hour shows in that kind of television. So, I've been very blessed working with quality work" (Reid).

There was one role, however, that Reid did not enjoy: "I had one bad experience in the past 11 years. I did 13 weeks at NBC [in the days] before *Cosby*, when they were in third place, called *Teacher's Only*. That was a horrible show. I tried my best to get off that show, but they wouldn't let me out of the contract. Talk about culture shock; leaving *KRP* and going to that is like getting out of motion pictures and getting dinner theater. It was really quite frightening....And I was thinking of quitting the business—[I thought,] 'If this is television I don't want to do it' " (Reid).

Fortunately, Reid remained in television, and in 1988 he became an integral part of what many TV critics consider to be one of TV's finest half-hour series, *Frank's Place*, produced by Wilson. Reid played a Boston professor of ancient civilization who was forced to take over his father's New Orleans bar, the Chez Louisian. Filmed through a sort of smoky haze and complete with a soundtrack filled with classic jazz and blues, the series seemed to capture the sound, look and feel of New Orleans. Though it ran for only one season, the episodes of *Frank's Place* were like excellent one-act plays that did not rely on "laugh-out-loud" humor. It is hard to classify *Frank's Place* as a sitcom. Filled with wit, pathos and honesty, it was an inventive show that provided an accurate portrayal of Black American life in New Orleans.

Reid feels that the realism of *Frank's Place* was because of Wilson's commitment to research. "We constantly researched," noted Reid. "That's another thing that the writers in this town won't do. It's almost this egotistical belief that *they* are reality. You know, there are a lot of people around here who write for television—they write it out of their minds and out of their conceptions of what is this world really like—the ghetto, or any [other] community. They don't even write that well for white America, no less black America.

"...You know, I see shows [concerning black families] where the mother works downtown at the urban center and they live in the suburbs—you never see their job...it takes place in the home. There was one with a woman in their home, but she worked in New York. They live way out, like an hour on the train. And they have episodes where kids come home from school and she's coming home from work. Well, we know that that's impossible. If she gets off at four in Manhattan, takes a train, she's gonna get home at dark,—six, or seven—and she's in no mood to come in and fix them no happy dinner. Well, to avoid that issue, they have ignored it—like she flies home by jet. I would use that, because in there is some comedy. 'What happened on the train today?' 'You fix your own dinner.' There's a lot that can go on, and if you're going to go that way, I would go with reality as a base, not [with] the make believe—the TV reality.

"So, I find that for Hugh Wilson—and he was my first mentor in television and producing—his thing was researching. Every year, every subject, every episode, [there was] something he would research...he'd bring in a specialist.

"On *Frank's Place*, he and I went to New Orleans on three separate occasions before he wrote the script—and researched—he *found* those characters. After we did the pilot, before Hugh went to work, he brought in a restaurant specialist whose job was to make a restaurant better. Hugh showed him the floor plan of this restaurant, and Hugh said 'Tell me how to make this successful?' The guy went about telling Hugh what was wrong with the restaurant. [The specialist] said 'Well your floor plan [is all wrong].' He told Hugh everything that was wrong.

"Well, everything [that he said] was wrong was a comedy episode. Because that's what Hugh wanted to hear...I can name at least five to ten

stories of *Frank's Place* that would be stories based on this [research].
Now who would think to do that? As a matter of fact, when Hugh told
the company that was financing the show that he was going to spend
$3,000 [on this restaurant specialist], they thought he was crazy. But that
$3,000 paid off" (Reid).

Not everyone liked *Frank's Place*, particularly members of racial
hate groups. Reid recalled how one racist wrote in to complain that
Frank's Place was a dangerous show because it "portrayed Blacks as
human beings." Instead of getting angry, Reid tried to find some humor
in the situation. "This guy had watched four shows," exclaimed Reid. "I
wish he had a meter!" (Reid).

Indeed, for all its moments, *Frank's Place* never attained sufficient
ratings to insure success. Reid feels that *Frank's Place* could have
survived had the network given it more of a chance. "*Frank's Place*
would have been successful had we been given another year. What hurt
Frank's Place, the reason that show is not on, was lack of understanding
on the network's part on how to promote the show. Also, [it was a
matter of] bad timing—right show, wrong time. The network itself was
going downhill into third place and losing—rapidly plunging. So,
nobody would watch that network to start with. So, where do you
promote this show? If nobody's watching the shows that you're
promoting your shows on, it becomes a catch-22.

"Thirdly, they changed the time on [*Frank's Place*]. Suddenly...
television is not stable. When I was a kid, you could count on everyday,
at a certain hour, a program coming on—unless there was an act of God
or a political problem. You could count on it. People shaped their lives
around it. Now a show is on and they move it around the schedule so
much—look at what happened to *Moonlighting*. It was on, it was pre-
empted, it was re-run—there's no consistency. If they had left [*Frank's
Place*] at a time slot and let it build—we moved—they moved that show
six times in one season. It's a record for a new show" (Reid).

Reid also had similar problems with his latest series *Snoops*, which
was also canceled after one season in 1990. *Snoops* was the first show
for which Reid served as Executive producer. Starring Reid and his wife
Daphne Maxwell Reid, who had also appeared in *WKRP*'s
"Circumstantial Evidence," it was a sophisticated crime drama loosely
based on the classic "Thin Man" series.

Wilson has had his own problems with series television, coming up with quality shows that simply can't find an audience. His latest venture was *The Amazing Teddy Z*, which was based on a true story of a young talent agency mail room clerk who, by chance, becomes the representative of the agency's top client. Despite their commercial problems, *Frank's Place* and *Teddy Z* were both well received by television critics.

In an attempt to make what Wilson has referred to as his "fuck you" money—money that can allow him to experiment with the type of shows he wants to do—Wilson produced the theatrical release, *Police Academy* (Christensen 38), never pretending that the film was of any great value or quality. Nevertheless, the film's success has helped him to become one of the most powerful and respected producers in Hollywood.

Loni Anderson has also enjoyed a great deal of success, and, since *WKRP*, she has starred in *Easy Money*, a sitcom, and *Partners in Crime*, an hour mystery/drama that also starred Linda Carter.

Rod Daniel, who had directed a number of *WKRP*'s, also directed for *Partners In Crime*, which was not renewed after its 13-episode run (Terrance 318). Anderson's private life became news in the late 1980s when she married actor Burt Reynolds, whom she met while working on *WKRP*. Their romance has made great copy for numerous muckraking tabloids. In 1989, Loni and Bert adopted a young boy named Quinton.

Jump has done a number of TV guest spots, including the very controversial role of a child molester in 1983s "The Bicycle Man," a two-part episode of *Different Strokes*. *WKRP* writer Blake Hunter, who had written the episode and went on to produce ABC's *Who's The Boss*, personally asked Jump to play the part. Deciding whether or not to take the role was one of the most difficult decisions of Jump's career. "First of all," explained Jump, "I hated the character. Second, as an actor playing a character like Arthur Carlson, it was a career gamble.

"[After I had decided to do the episode,] I had a local hardware man tell me, 'Well, buddy, you've ruined your career now.'

"I said, 'I don't believe that. The American people will know—be smart enough to know why I did it.'

"And, he said, 'Why did you do it?'

"I said, 'To help any child that would possibly come up against those circumstances, see them for what they are, and how to avoid them.'

"And he said, 'Well, good luck.' And, there were times where I wondered, 'Did I make the right choice?' (Jump).

Apparently, Jump had made the right choice. Though it was tough to get parts after "The Bicycle Man," Jump eventually began showing up in a number of other TV roles, including an appearance in *Second Edition*, a 1984 sitcom pilot for CBS. That was Jump's second pilot since leaving *WKRP*; before "The Bicycle Man," he had also won a supporting character role in *Great Day* (Terrance 175), another sitcom pilot for CBS. Jump has also played the grandfather on ABC's *Growing Pains*, which is produced by *WKRP* veteran Dan Guntzelman and Steve Marshall. In the late 1980s Jump also received the coveted commercial role of the Maytag repairman, which is sort of an American icon that was previously played by Jesse White.

Frank Bonner parlayed his directing experience into a going profession, and he has directed for *Frank's Place, Just the Ten of Us* (Bonner), and a number of other shows. Bonner also played the recurring role of Father Hargis in *Just the Ten of Us*. Sanders and Michael Fairman had written a TV movie that starred Dick Van Dyke and Sid Caesar. Though they had written the script before the beginning of *WKRP*, the movie was not broadcast until 1982 (Sanders). Sanders was also involved in the 1983 NBC pilot *The Invisible Woman*, and has guested on *Simon and Simon, Murder, She Wrote, Gloria, Alice, Newhart, Who's the Boss*, and *Love Boat* (Parish, Terrance 370).

In 1985, Gary Sandy was involved in the NBC pilot *Heart's Island* (Parish, Terrance 370). He has also done a number of guest appearances in *Murder, She Wrote* and Reid's *Snoops*. Jan Smithers has also kept busy with appearances in such shows as *Mike Hammer, Cover Up, The Fall Guy, Murder, She Wrote*, and *The Comedy Factory* (Parish, Terrance 388-89). Smithers is currently married to actor James Brolin of *Hotel* and *Marcus Welby* fame. Writer Tom Chehak went on to produce *Alien Nation* for the Fox Network and writers Peter Torokvei and Bill Dial have also been involved in a number of writing projects.

Edie McClurg, who had played Herb Tarlek's wife Lucille, most recently played the neighbor in *The Hogan Family*, and Allyn Ann McLerie, who played Carmen Carlson, appears as the mother in the Jay Tarses sitcom *The Days and Nights of Molly Dodd*.

Perhaps *WKRP*'s greatest success story is *WKRP* itself. Though it was never a sustained hit in prime time, it has enjoyed phenomenal success in syndication. "It got canceled," recalled Wilson, "and [MTM] thought, 'Well, we'll put it in syndication and see what happens.' Boom. And after a couple of years the thing had grossed over $100-million in syndication, which I believe is more than anything they've ever done. A show like *Hill Street*—they'll probably lose money on that. Those one-hour shows don't syndicate that well..." (Wilson).

Distributed by Victory Television, *WKRP* immediately became one of the hottest shows in syndication. Sold to 90 markets in 1982, it premiered in 28 of them that same year (Feuer, et al. 236). Even nine years after its cancellation, it still placed well, reportedly running in 47 markets covering 35 percent of the country in November 1989 (Mahoney 56). In 1990, *Entertainment Weekly* voted *WKRP* as the sixth most popular syndicated program of all time. Trying to explain the show's new found success, Sanders quipped that it was because people now knew where to find it.

It is a safe bet that viewers will continue to find *WKRP*, for many of its stories and characters have become firmly entrenched in our psyche and our popular culture. Who can think of Thanksgiving Day without the requisite airing of "Turkey's Away," the sitcom genre's holiday equivalent to *Miracle on 34th Street* and *It's a Wonderful Life*? Who can encounter a sleazy, tacky salesman without thinking of good old Herb Tarlek? Who can think of a rock-and-roll DJ without envisioning the face of Dr. Johnny Fever?

Because evaluating entertainment is such a subjective pursuit, it would be wrong to try and attach superlatives such as "best" or "greatest" to *WKRP*—or to any other sitcom, for that matter. That was never the purpose of this work. Rather, its purpose was to show that the original *WKRP* as one of those shows that, surrounded by a sea of banal sitcoms, has managed to make it to the shore of the small-yet-exclusive island of intelligent, meaningful and witty work. What is amazing in the case of *WKRP* is that it was able to reach that shore despite killer storms of bad network decisions and tremendous waves of critical indifference. In the long run, *WKRP*'s talent, dedication and honesty have served to anchor the sitcom's place in history—Indeed, *WKRP* has become America's favorite radio station.

Loni Anderson at her receptionist's desk. (From the Collection of Blake Hunter.)

Hugh Wilson plays a police officer in the "Hold Up" episode. Writers Tom Chehak and Blake Hunter join him. Gary Goodrow is the crook. (From the Collection of Blake Hunter.)

The ground crew prepares the W.W. I-era bi-plane for "The Airplane Show," the only *WKRP* episode filmed on-location in Cincinnati. (From the Collection of Blake Hunter.)

Out of respect for the series, the cast dressed in formal attire for the last Thursday camera-blocking day of the fourth season. According to Blake Hunter, the cast sensed the show would not be returning for a fifth season; they were right. (From the Collection of Blake Hunter.)

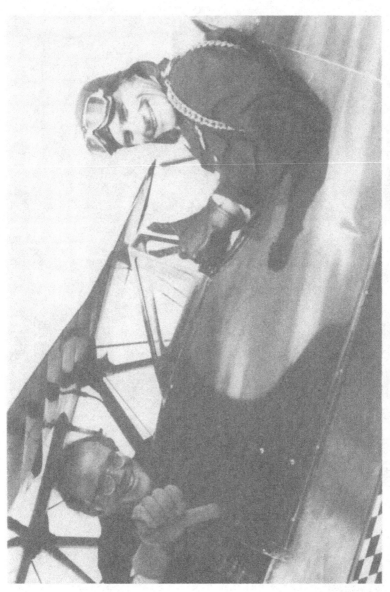

Richard Sanders and his writing partner, Michael Fairman, who played the over-the-edge pilot Buddy Baker in "The Airplane Show." Sanders actually went up in the plane for the episode's flight sequences. (From the Collection of Blake Hunter.)

Hugh Wilson hard at work on a rewrite. (From the Collection of Blake Hunter.)

Howard Hesseman as "Dr. Johnny Fever." (From the Collection of Blake Hunter.)

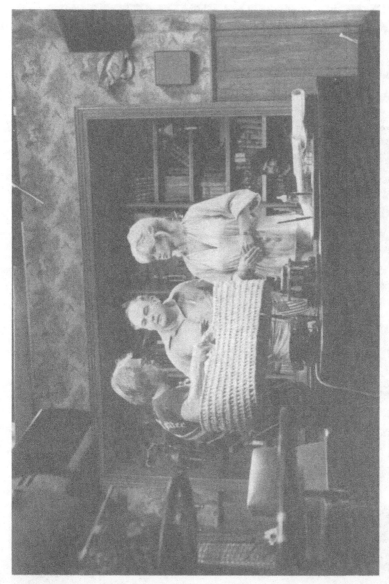

Howard Hesseman, Gordon Jump and Loni Anderson during camera-blocking on a Thursday before Friday's taping of the show. (From the Collection of Blake Hunter.)

Hugh Wilson makes a change in a scene in Mr. Carlson's office. (From the Collection of Blake Hunter.)

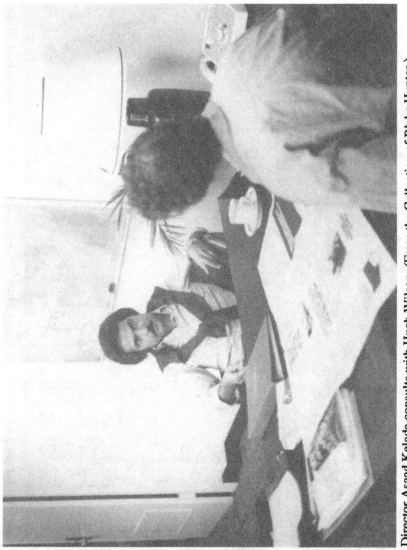

Director Asaad Kelada consults with Hugh Wilson. (From the Collection of Blake Hunter.)

Between shows the actors, writers and staff met in the green room to discuss rough spots in the first show and to make any changes that might be needed before the second show was taped. (From the Collection of Blake Hunter.)

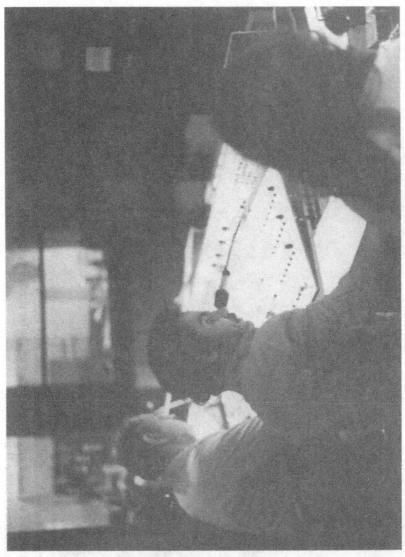

Director Asaad Kelada in the control booth during the taping of a show. (From the Collection of Blake Hunter.)

Hugh Wilson does the warmup for the audience who came to see the taping. His opening was always the same, "Welcome to Cincinnati, Ladies and Gentlemen." (From the Collection of Blake Hunter.)

"Living on the Air in Cincinnati"
The Episode Guide to WKRP

The following guide is based on the author's viewing of the broadcast syndicated versions of all 90 WKRP episodes. Additional information for this guide was obtained through the author's interviews with the cast and production crew, along with information from a promotional episode guide provided by Victory television.

	Credits
Andy Travis	Gary Sandy
Arthur C. Carlson	Gordon Jump
Johnny Fever	Howard Hesseman
Jennifer Marlowe	Loni Anderson
Venus Flytrap	Tim Reid
Herbert R. Tarlek	Frank Bonner
Les Nessman	Richard Sanders
Bailey Quarters	Jan Smithers
Created by	Hugh Wilson
Original Music	Tom Welle

The First Season—1978-1979

Episode 0001
"Pilot"
Written by Hugh Wilson
Directed by Jay Sandrich

In the words of DJ Johnny Caravella, WKRP in Cincinnati is "rock bottom." Playing music that is 20 years out of date, the station is losing $100,000 a year and foundering in the Cincinnati market. Run by the somewhat scatter-brained fishing fanatic Arthur Carlson, the station is owned by Carlson's mother, a heartless, domineering woman who loves money and hates rock and roll.

Enter Andy Travis, the new program director, who promises that his proposed rock format will allow the station to break even in the first year and make $800,000 the next. Carlson reluctantly gives Travis a free hand. Although Momma is initially upset, Andy convinces her to give it a try.

Additional Cast

Momma Carlson   Sylvia Sidney

Episode 0002
"Pilot Part II"
Written by Hugh Wilson
Directed by Michael Zinberg

It has been two weeks since the format change and Andy is having his share of problems; not only has he been fighting with Momma Carlson, Herb Tarlek and Les Nessman—poor Andy can't even find his laundry. WKRP has steadily been losing some of its oldest accounts, including Shady Hills Rest Home, Rolling Thunder European Regularity Tonic, and Bo-Peep Safety Shoes. Without any money to spend on promoting the format change, Andy solicits ideas for publicity stunts.

137

Meanwhile, a group of older citizens have assembled in the WKRP lobby to protest the format change. They not only demand the return of their elevator music, but also they want an on-air apology to Lawrence Welk. Andy quickly realizes that these old people are the key to the publicity stunt he has been looking for.

Additional Cast

Wayne R. Coe	Richard Stahl
Mrs. Burstyn	Nedra Volz
Buzzy Milker	Delos V. Smith

Episode 0003
"Preacher"
Written by Bill Dial
Directed by Michael Zinberg

In the opinion of the Greater Cincinnati Inter-Religious Council, WKRP's Reverend Little Ed Pembrook, the 300-pound ex-wrestler who is now the leader of "The Church of the Mighty Struggle," has overstepped the bounds of "good taste, good sense, and good religion." Little Ed is selling cheap religious artifacts such as John the Baptist Shower Curtains and Dead Sea Scroll Steak Knives on his hour long, 8:00 am Sunday radio show. The question facing Andy and Carlson: How do you tell the man who once threw Haystack Calhoun out of a wrestling ring and into a soda pop machine that he is through?

Additional Cast

Rev. Little Ed Pembrook	Michael Keenan
Sister of Mercy #1	Mary Steel Smith
Sister of Mercy #2	Cynthia Szigeti
Sister of Mercy #3	Suzanne Kent
Rev. Drinkwater	John Chappel
Father Riley	Arthur Malet
Rabbi Fishbein	Jeremiah Morris

Episode 0004
"Hoodlum Rock"
Written by Hugh Wilson
Directed by Michael Zinberg

What is the difference between punk rock and hoodlum rock? According to the band Scum of the Earth, punk rockers dress deplorably and they do not physically attack their audience. Regardless of this, Andy thinks that Scum will make a perfect first concert for WKRP to promote. Though the band members appear to be more trouble then they are worth, the concert pays off in the end.

Additional Cast

Steve Pievy	Ned Wertimer
Blood	Peter Elbling
Dog	Michael Des Barres
Sir Nigel Weatherbee	Jim Henderson
Waiter	Chick Waters

Original music by DETECTIVE

Episode 0005
"Les on a Ledge"
Written by Hugh Wilson
Directed by Asaad Kelada

What happens when one of journalism's most "trusted" voices gets accused of being a homosexual and is banned from doing sports reports from the stadium locker room? This is the problem that faces Les Nessman, five-time winner of the Buckeye News Hawk award.

Convinced his career is over, Les steps out on the ledge of Carlson's office and, quoting from Hamlet, contemplates suicide. Although everyone tries their best to bring Les back in, it takes an apology from the baseball player who had Nessman banned.

Watch for this episode's teaser: In one of the most famous Nessman scenes, Les refers to golfer Chi Chi Rodriguez as "Chi' Chi' Rod-wa-gweeze."

Episode 0006
"Bailey's Show"
Written by Joyce Armor and Judie Neer
Directed by Asaad Kelada

The shy, yet ambitious, Bailey has been given the opportunity to produce a public affairs program called "Cincinnati Beat." After getting Johnny to agree to host the program, Bailey faces one major obstacle— finding a suitable guest that has something worthwhile to say.

Additional Cast

Dr. Hyman Monroe	Woodrow Parfrey
Mrs. Woodruff	Kathryn Ish
Roxanne	Casey Brown
Mr. Eisenhower	Berry Kroeger

Episode 0007
"Hold Up"
Written by Tom Chehak
Directed by Asaad Kelada

Finally, Herb has found a potential advertising client that fits WKRP's new rock format. Del Murdoch, the fast-talking, ever-hyper owner of Del's Stereo and Sound is one salesman who is perhaps even less scrupulous than Herb. Del's motto: "No refunds."

Though Herb makes the sale, which includes a live remote, things rapidly fall apart. Station Engineer Bucky Rouse destroys some of Del's shoddy Japanese merchandise. When they start the remote, the power goes out. Once they get back on the air, the only customer who shows up ends up being an out of work DJ who hijacks the show.

This is the first show to mention that WKRP was the 16th station in an 18 station market; it also noted that WPIG was Cincinnati's number one station.

Additional Cast

Del Murdoch	Hamilton Camp
Bucky Dornster	Bill Dial
Bob Burnatt	Gary Goodrow

Policeman #1	Hugh Wilson
Other cop	Tom Chehak
Other cop	Blake Hunter

Episode 0008
"Turkey's Away"
Written by Bill Dial
Directed by Michael Zinberg

It is 45 degrees and cloudy in Cincinnati, and poor Arthur Carlson is feeling dejected. Even though he is the station manager, he is not "allowed" to do anything. Jennifer keeps him from all the important calls and mail, Herb and Les brush off his questions with curt responses, and all Fever can do is deliver sarcastic comments.

Making his stand, Carlson decides to take total control of the station, including promotions. Coming up with an idea that he says will make radio history, Carlson, Herb and Les prepare for their infamous turkey drop. When the turkeys end up plummeting to the ground like "sacks of wet cement," all Carlson can say is: "As God as my witness, I thought Turkeys could fly."

WKRP's most famous episode, this was one of the first to clearly define the split that existed between Les, Herb, and Carlson and the station's "more casually dressed" employees. This rift would be explored more fully in later episodes, as well.

It also features the classic scene in which Les patterns his description of the Turkey drop after the famous Hindenburg crash report.

Episode 0009
"Goodbye Johnny"
Written by Blake Hunter
Directed by Asaad Kelada

It is a 14-degree, windy, snowy day, but even the weather can not mar Dr. Fever's spirits; while Cincinnati digs out of its vicious snowstorm, Fever plays "Surfin' USA." It is not just part of his "Seasonal Cincinnati Snow Shoe Stomp." Indeed, thanks to poetic justice, Fever is L.A. Bound; he has received a job offer from the top competitor of the L.A. station that fired him.

Instead of being happy, the rest of the crew is upset at the prospect of losing Fever. Throwing him a farewell party, the gang hopes to convince Fever to stay. Touched as he is, Fever takes the L.A. job.

A number of little trivia items are presented in this episode, including Fever's original salary, which was $17,500. It was also the first episode to feature Edie McClurg as Herb's wife.

By the way, what was Les Nessman's regular topic for the Speechmaker's club? "The Red Menace in Our Own Backyard."

Additional Cast

Lucille Tarlek	Edie McClurg
Waitress	Janet Meshad

Episode 0010
"Johnny Comes Back"
Written by Blake Hunter
Directed by Asaad Kelada

With Fever gone, this continuation of "Goodbye Johnny" has Andy looking for a new replacement for the morning drive time. Against his better judgment, Andy agrees to audition Doug Winner, a DJ suggested by sleazy record promoter Murray Gressler. After Andy hires Winner, Fever returns to WKRP—he got fired from the L.A. job for swearing on the air. When Fever recounts the story of his ouster to the gang, he repeats the obscenity that got him fired. Though it is bleeped out in the episode, Hesseman recalls that he either said "fuck you" or "tough shit."

Unable to place Fever in drive time, Andy gives Johnny the midnight to 6:00 am slot. However, when it is discovered that Winner is a coke addict being supplied by Gressler, Winner is fired and Fever regains his show.

Watch for Sam Anderson playing Mason Nobel, his first of many character roles for the series.

Additional Cast

Doug Winner	Philip Charles MacKenzie
Murray Gressler	Jeff Altman
Mason Nobel	Sam Anderson

Episode 0011
"Love Returns"
Written by Bill Dial
Directed by Asaad Kelada

Although the series was originally going to concentrate more on the Andy Travis character, this is one of the few episodes that actually did. When Andy's ex-girlfriend Linda Taylor, now a big pop singer, stops into Cincinnati for a concert, Andy and Linda rekindle their old flame. As things heat up for the former lovers, Andy must decide whether to keep his job at WKRP or pursue a full-time relationship with Linda.

Meanwhile, Fever and Venus try their luck at picking a suitable winner for the station's "Win a Date with a DJ" contest. Venus fares okay with his date, but Fever winds up with a guy named Kim.

This episode also features the first appearance of Les's mobile News Gathering Unit (a motor scooter) and the first reference to Carlson's wife Carmen.

Additional Cast

Linda Taylor	Barrie Youngfellow
Howard R. Sternworthy	Hugh Gillin
Roadie Ray	Mickey McMeel

Episode 0012
"I Want to Keep My Baby"
Written by Hugh Wilson
Directed by Asaad Kelada

An unwed teenage mother who feels that she has no one else in the world to turn to leaves her baby with Dr. Fever. Wanting to give the mother a chance to come back for the baby, Fever and the rest of the gang take care of the little girl.

Additional Cast

Mrs. Brown	Mary Betten
Mr. Hudspeth	Michael Flanagan
The Baby	Danny Openden

Episode 0013
"Fish Story"
Written by Hugh Wilson
under the name "Raoul Plager"
Directed by Asaad Kelada

Andy picks the worse day for a reporter to visit the station. Venus and Fever are involved in an on-air drunk driving campaign that goes awry. Herb, running around in a giant Carp suit, along with Les and Bailey, wind up in jail, and the WPIG pig mascot destroys the WKRP lobby.

Additional Cast

Pig	Lee Bergere
Officer Plyler	Jerry Hardin
Quentin Stone	M.G. Kelly
The Painter	Jack O'Leary
Student #1	Francis Sermier
Student #2	Fred Fisher
Student #3	Marty Halfond
Student #4	Michael Carpita
Student #5	Lief Bristow
Security Officer	Steven Wright

Episode 0014
"The Contest Nobody Could Win"
Written by Casey Piotrowski
Directed by Asaad Kelada

When Fever accidentally misreads a memo and tells his listeners that they can win $5,000 in the station's "Mystery Music Contest,"—the prize was supposed to be $50—Andy and the gang must come up with a contest that would be impossible to win. Despite their stringing six short snatches of songs that would be seemingly impossible to discern, the second caller correctly names the songs.

When Herb convinces Carlson that the foul-up was because of the inherent difference between "the suits" and "the dungarees," (another reference to the old and new guard at WKRP), Carlson decides to take over all promotions, including the presentation of the $5,000. However, when "the suits" hand the money over to a con man, it is Fever to the rescue.

The songs used in the contest were: "Too Wild to Tame," by The Boys; "Tumbling Dice," by the Stones; "YMCA" by the Village People; "Dankeschoene" by Wayne Newton; "Straight On" by Heart; and "The Star Spangled Banner."

Additional Cast

Don Pesola #1	Vincent Schiavelli
Don Pesola #2	Tracey Walter
Photographer #1	Ken Hill
Photographer #2	Gary Devaney

Episode 0015
"Mama's Review"
Written by Hugh Wilson
Directed by Asaad Kelada

Arthur Carlson, who has been manager of WKRP since 1955, is nervously awaiting the arrival of his mother. Saying he would rather face a Sumo wrestler than one of his mother's quarterly reviews, Carlson warns Andy that, before the meeting is over, Momma will either cut the budget or fire somebody.

Through a series of flashbacks, Arthur and Andy go on to justify some of the strange occurrences at WKRP. This was the first episode aired after the mid-season hiatus, and the first to feature Carol Bruce in the recurring role of Lillian Carlson.

Additional Cast

Momma Carlson	Carol Bruce

Episode 0016
"A Date with Jennifer"
Written by Richard Sanders & Michael Fairman
Directed by Asaad Kelada

It is 57 degrees and cloudy, but the world is a bright place for Les Nessman, who has just been chosen to receive the coveted Silver Sow Award from the Peter Piper Pork Packer's Guild. One problem—Les needs a date for the award banquet.

Much to Herb's dismay, Jennifer agrees to accompany Les. However, when Herb convinces the Big Guy to institute a policy against employee dating, Les has to decide whether or not to defy the new orders.

This was the first episode to feature Les' tape-outline office, with the tape representing the walls that Les felt his newsroom should have.

Additional Cast
Mr. Macho Announcer (V.O.)   Brad Crandall

Episode 0017
"Tornado"
Written by Blake Hunter
Directed by Will MacKenzie

No one takes Les seriously when he insists that the station should be more concerned with civil defense preparation. However, when a series of tornadoes strike the Cincinnati area, the staff quickly changes their opinion. When Andy is knocked unconscious from the wreckage of a broken window, it is up to Les and Carlson to lead the team. Leaving behind the group of Japanese tourist who are visiting the station, Carlson proves his mettle when he saves the life of a little girl during a live phone call.

Additional Cast
Jose Rodriguez   Rene Enriquez
1st Japanese Executive   David Chow
2nd Japanese Executive   Bill Saito

Episode 0018
"Young Master Carlson"
Written by Blake Hunter and Hugh Wilson
Directed by Will MacKenzie

The Big Guy is having a problem with his "little guy;" Arthur's 11-year-old son has run away from Prussian Valley Military School to live with Momma Carlson, who suggests that Arthur find a job at the station for Little Arthur. When the child proves to be nothing more than a sexist, bigoted terror, The Big Guy has to lay down the law—a chore that does not come easy to Carlson.

Additional Cast

Momma Carlson	Carol Bruce
Arthur Carlson, Jr.	Sparky Marcus

Episode 0019
"Never Leave Me, Lucille"
Written by Bill Dial
Directed by Asaad Kelada

Les gets a surprise in the bullpen as he goes through his morning exercise routine—Herb, who has spent the night at the station, has left his wife Lucille. Les desperately tries to change Herb's mind, but to no avail. Telling Andy that the break-up is permanent, Herb calls on the intercom to Jennifer and tells her that he is a free man. Jennifer, her worst fear realized, quickly hangs up in terror.

When Fever draws the short-straw and gets custody of Herb—and Herb's "Bullfighter on Velvet" painting—the rest of the unmarried boys show Herb how rotten single life is; they eventually convince Herb to go back to Lucille.

Additional Cast

Lucille Tarlek	Edie McClurg
Bartender	Jim Begg

Episode 0020
"A Commercial Break"
Written by Richard Sanders and Michael Fairman
Directed by Rod Daniel

How can WKRP say no to $600 a day in advertising revenue? That is the problem facing Andy and Carlson when Ferryman's Funerals, one of the largest funeral home chains in the nation, wants to place a hip, upbeat ad campaign with the station. At first the gang is very enthusiastic, coming up with a catchy jingle to sell Ferryman's pre-need service. Carlson thinks the spot is in bad taste, and, as much as he regrets it, turns down Ferryman's $18,000 advance on the contract.

Additional Cast

Randall Ferryman   Fred Stutham

Episode 0021
"I Do, I Do...For Now"
Written by Tom Chehak
Directed by Will Mackenzie

Jennifer is surprised when T.J. Watson, her old boyfriend from her hometown of Rock Throw, West Virginia, shows up to cash in on an old debt—the lovely Jennifer Elizabeth once promised to marry T.J. Desperate to get the guitar picking, good-old-boy off her back, she claims that she is already married—to Johnny Fever.

T.J.—a man not to be toyed with—is not easily dissuaded. He decides to stay around to see that everything is fine between Fever and Jennifer. When the gang assembles for a little party at Jennifer's apartment, they discover that T.J. is actually a very talented singer. In the meantime, T.J. discovers that Jennifer has been lying about her marriage to Fever. Though he does not get the girl, T.J. does end up getting his song recorded.

Trivia: The doorbell to Jennifer's luxury apartment plays "Fly Me To The Moon."

Special Guest Star

T.J. Watson   Hoyt Axton

Additional Cast

Man in Elevator   Buzz Sapien

Episode 0022
"Who is Gordon Sims?"
Written by Tom Chehak
Directed by Rod Daniel

When Venus refuses to let Herb and Les take a picture of him for a promotional advertisement, the whole WKRP staff begins to wonder what is wrong. Realizing that they do not even know the DJ's real name, Les and Herb begin to suspect that Venus is hiding something—and they are right: Venus, a/k/a Gordon Sims, was a Vietnam deserter.

Though Venus' first instinct is to cut and run, Carlson convinces the DJ to turn himself into the Army and take his chances. Tired of running, Venus reluctantly agrees. When it comes out that Venus actually deserted after completing his combat duty, the investigating officer finds that a general discharge is in order. Though he has to remain on the base for a couple of weeks while the paper work is processed, Venus—and Gordon Sims—are finally free.

Additional Cast

Major Hunter   Nicholas Worth

The Second Season—1979-1980

Episode 0023
"Baseball"
Written and Directed by Hugh Wilson

Les, whose violin lessons had robbed him of an athletically active childhood, has accepted a softball game challenge from Clark Callahan, the blow-hard station manager from WPIG AM & FM. Reluctantly, the rest of the gang decides to take on the PIGs.

During the game, Les is shifted from position to position. He is not the only one with problems; Arthur "Moose" Carlson struggles desperately to reclaim his illustrious college baseball past—he would like to hit the ball. Down nine to zip, Jennifer begins distracting the WPIG players as the rest of the WKRP gang picks up the pace. The score tied, it is up to "The Moose" and Les to save the day.

Except for the teaser, the entire episode was shot on location with remote camera work by Marvin Rush. Clark Callahan was played by Ross Bickell, who was Loni Anderson's husband at the time of the taping—Ross had been one of the hopefuls who had tried out for the part of Andy Travis.

Additional Cast

Bucky Dornster	Bill Dial
Clark Callahan	Ross Bickell
Umpire	Wyatt Johnson

Episode 0024
"Jennifer Falls in Love"
Written by Paul Hunter
Directed by Will MacKenzie

It is not a good day at WKRP for either Les or Jennifer. Les, who found out that he is the lowest paid broadcast journalist in town, wants a raise. Jennifer's problem is not as easy to understand—for the first time in her life, she is really in love. Her new man is blonde, beautiful and "every girl's dream." What's the problem? "He's poor!"

In the beginning, Jennifer's romance goes well—she and Steel Hawthorne are a handsome couple and have meaningful discussions on topics such as the sort of toothpaste they use. When Steel asks Jennifer to loan him $200 to fix his van, the relationship ends. Hurt that Steel has done to her what she does to other men, Jennifer becomes very depressed. Carlson, however, makes her feel better, noting that Jennifer, unlike Steel, never asks for favors.

Meanwhile, figuring there is strength in numbers, Les gets Venus to join with him in a demand for a raise. Venus gets the raise, but all Les gets is the gate. In the end, however, all is well when Andy and Carlson each give Les an additional $10 a week.

Additional Cast

Steel Hawthorne   Thomas Calloway

Episode 0025
"Carlson for President"
Written by Jim Paddock
Directed by Will MacKenzie

In an attempt to impress his mother, Arthur decides to run for the Cincinnati City Council. Andy, pleased at the prospect of having Carlson help the city instead of WKRP, quickly offers to do anything to help Carlson win. With Herb as the campaign manager, however, the campaign becomes an uphill battle.

Although Bailey uncovers the fact that Carlson's chief opponent Charles Tillman is a heavy drinker—he once fell face forward into a plate of lasagna at a "Friends of Armenia Dinner"—she makes Carlson promise not to use that information during an upcoming TV debate. During the debate, however, when Tillman attacks Carlson's clown-like make-up job—a sort of reversal on the Nixon-Kennedy debate—Carlson accidentally spills the beans about Tillman's drinking.

After that bombshell, Carlson begins to lead in the polls. Not wanting to win that way, Carlson begins to sabotage his own campaign, putting out posters with a mean-looking pose, insulting members of various civic groups, and making it appear that he has beaten his wife. In the end, The Big Guy loses the election big time.

Additional Cast

Charles Tillman	Howard Witt
Mitzi Monahan	Lillian Garrett-Bonner
Wendel Brooks	Howard Morton
Barry Schifrin	Dick McGarvin

Episode 0026
Episode 0027
"For Love or Money, Part I"
"For Love or Money, Part II"
Written by Mary Maguire
Directed by Will MacKenzie

Deciding to take control of the situation, shy Bailey asks Johnny out for a date. Johnny agrees to go. However, when Buffy Denver, an old flame from Johnny's L.A. days, calls to arrange a meeting, Johnny forgets all about the plans he made with Bailey.

Hoping to impress Buffy, Fever, on Herb's advice, gets the loan of Jennifer's apartment for the evening. This proves to be a mistake, for the luxurious apartment only feeds Buffy's real desire—to sue Johnny for palimony. As Fever feels the rope tighten around his neck, poor Bailey, stood up by Fever, waits at the station.

Additional Cast

Buffy Denver	Julie Payne

Episode 0028
"Bad Risk"
Written by Gene Fournier and Tom Joachim
Directed by Will MacKenzie

This episode proves the common law that only one thing in life is certain—at one point, someone you know will end up selling life insurance. When Herb Tarlek starts moonlighting for the Associated

Amalgamated Company, Ltd. Insurance Company, the staff runs for cover—all except Les Nessman, who, in one of his famous deep depressions, becomes Herb's first victim.

Herb sells Les a ton of insurance—including insurance on a boat that Herb also sold to Les. When the newsman crashes his mobile news scooter through the front window of a luck-less British couple, all Herb cares about is finding out whether Les mailed in the policy—unfortunately for Herb, Les did.

Depressed that he put the poor couple in the hospital, Les goes to visit them. At first they do not want to see Les, but, after they learn about the insurance, they all become good friends, except for Herb, who loses his job with the insurance company.

Additional Cast

J. Garrett Hopkins	William Glover
Tiffany Hopkins	Helena Carroll

Episode 0029
"Put Up or Shut Up"
Written by Blake Hunter, Steve Marshall,
& Steven Kampmann
Directed by Will MacKenzie

Herb, who has entered the WKRP lobby singing "If You Think I'm Sexy," is being more relentless than ever in his pursuit of Jennifer. His wife and children have gone to Lucille's mother's house for ten days, and Herb is on the prowl. With a musical promise to Jennifer that "Our Day Will Come," Herb walks back to the bullpen leaving Jennifer in shock.

Bailey suggests that Jennifer call Herb's bluff. Balking at first, Jennifer decides to give it a try. When Herb takes the lovely Ms. Marlowe up on her offer, Jennifer is at her wit's end.

Maybe Bailey was right; indeed, Herb begins to have second thoughts about going out with Jennifer. When Les tells Herb that the whole thing is just a plan to call the salesman's bluff, however, Herb decides to go through with the date. Nevertheless, once he is at the apartment, all Herb can do is hyperventilate and sweat. In a touching moment, Herb—with Jennifer's tactful help—decides that if he and Jennifer can not be lovers, at least they can be friends.

This is also the episode in which Fever has problems with LSD flashbacks. Finally getting over the flashbacks, Fever has a quick relapse at the end of the episode when he sees Herb and Jennifer singing "I Love You Just the Way You Are."

Episode 0030
"Baby, If You've Ever Wondered"
Written by Bill Dial
Directed by Rod Daniel

It's a scary day at WKRP—The Arbitron ratings book has arrived, their fate packaged in "a plain brown wrapper." Carlson is afraid to open it. Telling the others to leave the office, Andy and Carlson begin to check out the numbers.

Surprisingly, the news is good. For the first time in seven years, WKRP's numbers have gone up instead of down, and the station has moved from 16th to 14th place. Fever and Venus, who showed the best numbers, along with the rest of the gang, are pleased, all except for Andy, who feels that the format change alone would have accounted for the two place move. Becoming depressed, Andy feels that he has not accomplished anything in his year at the station.

Sensing Andy's frustration, Venus gets to the heart of the problem. It seems that Andy is caught between his desire to make the station prosper and his affection for some of the station's less-than-perfect employees, namely Herb, Les, and Carlson. Saying that Andy can not fire the little guys without firing the Big Guy—and Carlson can't be fired because his Momma owns the station—Venus convinces Andy that WKRP is more than just a place of business; it is a family. Tired of "packing and unpacking up and down the dial," Andy realizes that WKRP, for better or worse, is his home.

Trivia—The Numbers Game: While Venus and Fever had good numbers overall, Les had lost six percent of his 65-and-older audience. By the way, Herb's commission on sales was five percent, and Carlson also got a ten percent cut for each spot sold.

Episode 0031
"The Patter of Little Feet"
Written by Blake Hunter
Directed by Will MacKenzie

As Arthur prepares for an expensive fishing trip in which he plans to stalk the elusive Bonefish, his wife Carmen drops by with a surprise—she is pregnant. Stunned, Carlson does not know how to react—after all, Carmen is over 40. However, realizing how much they both want another child, Arthur and Carmen agree that it is good news.

Momma does not agree—she is concerned about Carmen's health and wants Arthur to tell Carmen to have an abortion. Coming up with a number of good reasons to follow his mom's advice, in the end Arthur and Carmen opt to let nature take its course.

Great moment: After Arthur and Carmen resolve the question of abortion, Carlson asks Venus to play something soft and sweet. Reluctantly, Venus plays "We've Only Just Begun." As the Carlsons dance in Arthur's office, Venus sits in the booth, staring in disbelief at the spinning Carpenters album.

Additional Cast

Carmen Carlson   Allyn Ann McLerie
Momma Carlson   Carol Bruce

Episode 0032
"God Talks to Johnny"
Written by Hugh Wilson
Directed by Will MacKenzie

Fever is sure that God is talking to him—requesting that Fever, of all things, become a golf pro. Soon, the rest of the staff begins to doubt Fever's sanity, and Fever himself begins to think he is going crazy. Checking into a hospital, Fever is met by Carlson, who has come down to talk with Johnny. Saying that there is nothing wrong with hearing God's voice, Carlson sets a worried Fever at ease.

Episode 0033
"Bailey's Big Break"
Written by Steve Marshall
Directed by Will MacKenzie

Andy is listening to audition tapes for a second newscaster, much to Les' dismay. When Bailey presents an audition tape of her own, Les just laughs, but Andy likes the tape and gives Bailey the job.

As the days go by, however, Les keeps Bailey busy with menial chores, denying her a chance to go on the air. Bailey takes the matter to Andy, who orders Les to let Bailey deliver a newscast. When Bailey proves to be more than competent, Andy decides to give her a few regular broadcasts of her own. Les falls into a deep depression.

Not wanting to hurt Les any longer, Bailey decides to back out of the job. Ashamed of how he has acted, however, Les convinces Bailey to continue doing the news.

Episode 0034
"Mike Fright"
Written by Dan Guntzelman
Directed by Will MacKenzie

Dr. Fever, upset about the five-week-old garbage strike afflicting Cincinnati, suggests that his listeners dump their trash outside of city hall. When Fever learns that upwards of 300 people have taken his advice —plunging the station into legal trouble—he becomes aware of his own power and develops a case of mike fright.

As he is drowning his sorrows at Snookies bar, Fever is confronted by Andy, Venus, and Bailey, who try to convince Fever to go back on the air. Repeating the advice that Fever once gave her, Bailey tells Fever to pretend that he is talking to only one person. Back on the air, Fever apologizes for the trouble he started. The problem resolved, Fever again gets carried away and tells his listeners to dump their garbage at the Mayor's house.

Trivia: WKRP's lawyer in this episode was the tiny Elgar Neece, played by Christian Seaborn. In the fourth season episodes "Pills" and "Circumstantial Evidence," actor Max Wright played WKRP lawyer Frank Bartman.

Episode 0035
"Les' Groupie"
Written by Steve Marshall
Story by Paul Hunter
Directed by Rod Daniel

When a sexy female named Darlene calls into the booth asking for a date with one of WKRP's on-air personalities, everyone is surprised to find out that Les is the object of the fan's affection. Les does not know what to do, but on Fever's insistence, the newsman decides to take a chance.

Though he is flattered at first by the attention, Darlene, who moves in with Les, makes the newscaster's life a living hell. Les struggles to tell Darlene it is over, but he cannot seem to summon the courage to do so. When Darlene stops by the office and pulls up Les' tape-outline office "walls," however, Les lets his anger do the talking.

Trivia: This episode noted that Les had a vicious dog named Phil, which helped to answer the question why Les Nessman always had a bandage—Phil was tearing poor Les apart.

Episode 0036
"A Family Affair"
Written by Tim Reid
Directed by Rod Daniel

Andy's sister Carol is in town and Andy wants Fever to take her out. Being the good guy that he is, Fever agrees—especially since Andy is willing to pay the DJ $50 for the favor. However, when Venus arrives at the station, he and Carol hit it off rather well and Venus decides to show Carol around the Queen City.

When Andy discovers that Venus is out with Carol, he begins to get upset—especially when Venus does not show up for his air shift.

When Venus and Carol finally return to the station, Venus and Andy get into an argument. Realizing that he is being a bigot, Andy apologizes and invites Venus and Carol over to Snookies. In an attempt to prove that he really is not prejudiced, Andy insists that Venus dance with Carol. Snookies, however, is not exactly a bastion of racial understanding. As Venus and Carol dance, a redneck tries to stop them. Preserving his dignity, Venus, along with Andy, punch the racist's lights out.

Additional Cast

Carol Travis	Allison Argo
Redneck	Don Pulford

Episode 0037
"Jennifer's Home For Christmas
Written by Dan Guntzelman and Steve Marshall
Directed by Rod Daniel

In their first Christmas episode, the gang begins to fear that Jennifer is going to be alone for the holidays. With only the best of intentions, each of the WKRP staff drop by and bring Jennifer a present—a Christmas tree. Sitting amongst the make-shift forest of holiday cheer, Jennifer announces that she has to leave—she is going to spend Christmas in Bethlehem.

An interesting bit of business in this episode involves Johnny, who slowly gets loaded on the holiday punch in Jennifer's apartment. Also note that series writer/producer Steve Marshall plays a bit role as a delivery man.

Additional Cast

Henri	George Gaynes
Delivery Man #1	Don Diamond
Delivery Man #2	Steve Marshall

Episode 0038
"Sparky"
Written by Peter Torokvei & Steven Kampmann
Directed by Rod Daniel

Les is upset when Andy hires former Cincinnati Red's Manager Sparky Anderson for the station's new sports talk show. Les gets the last laugh when Sparky's show fails miserably. When Carlson and Andy confront Sparky with the news, Sparky says, "Every time I come into this town I get fired."

This episode was filled with a number of great comic moments. When Jennifer says that she never missed a Reds game Sparky coached, Sparky surprises the lovely Ms. Marlowe by reciting the exact box (110), row (6), and seat number (8) in which she sat.

There is further fun in Sparky's interview with Derek Doogle, the captain of the Cincinnati Skids indoor soccer team who seems more obsessed with food than sports.

Hugh Gillin, who played WPIG's Howard Sternworthy in "Love Returns," makes his second guest appearance as the owner of Sunlux Petroleum, Sparky's sponsor.

Special Guest Star
Sparky Anderson   Himself

Additional Cast
Derek Doogle   Andrew Bloch
Cal Owens   Hugh Gillin

Episode 0039
"The Americanization of Ivan"
Story by Hugh Wilson
Written by Dan Guntzelman & Steve Marshall
Directed by Hugh Wilson

If there are two things in this world that Les knows about, they are hogs and communists. Thus, when a delegation of Russian hog experts pay Cincinnati a visit, Les promises to give the "commies" a little taste of "capitalistic journalism."

Fearing the worst, Andy has Bailey go along with Les to the conference. Ivan, the leader of the delegation, quickly develops a crush on Bailey and asks her to help him defect.

Bailey brings Ivan back to the station. Andy, thinking his life is not exciting, is thrilled at the opportunity to help the Soviet defect. However, they quickly learn that you cannot defect in Cincinnati; Cincinnati's U.S. Immigration Office's branch is too small—indeed, the office still has a picture of President Nixon. "They never sent me a Carter," explains Mr. Anderson, the branch officer played by Sam Anderson (his second character role in the series).

Back at the station, Bailey and Andy decide to drive Ivan to the Cleveland Immigration office. Before they can leave, the rest of the delegation arrives. Ivan tells the rest of the committee that he was merely posing as Andy and Bailey's friend to see the "capitalistic exploiters" first hand. However, when he tells the group to prepare to leave for Cleveland—their next stop—Ivan makes it clear that he still plans to defect.

Though the Russian jokes and dialogue ("Come along, you nin-com-poopies," etc.) seem a bit dated today, they were still fresh in 1979.

Additional Cast

Ivan Popasonaviski	Michael Pataki
Interpreter	Alex Rodine
Mr. Anderson	Sam Anderson

Episode 0040
"Herb's Dad"
Written by Peter Torokvei and Steven Kampmann
Directed by Rod Daniel

Herb has arranged a great deal with Shady Hills Rest Home—he will get Andy to run their tasteless spots and they will keep Herb's dad for a reasonable rate. When Herb Tarlek Sr., a retired salesman who dresses in the same tasteless fashion as Herb, arrives at the station, he makes it clear to his son that he has no intention of spending another minute at that "Shady Place."

Although Herb tries to get his dad to go back to the home, it is to no avail. In the end, Herb agrees to let his dad take up with a 33-year-old nurse and go out to California—Herb even gives his dad a little "pin money" to begin the trip.

Trivia: Herb collects salt and pepper shakers that his dad used to bring him after coming home from sales trips. Also, the dollar bill Tarlek Sr. used to win his liar's poker hand with Venus and Fever has six "nines."

Comeuppance: Soon after Parks taped this episode, he was fired from the Miss America Pageant. In August 1990, it was announced that Parks had been rehired to appear on the program to sing the "Miss America" theme.

Special Guest Star
Herb Tarlek, Sr.   Bert Parks

Episode 0041
"The Doctor's Daughter"
Written by Lissa Levin
Directed by Frank Bonner

Laurie Caravella, Johnny's daughter, whom he has not seen in twelve years, shows up at the station. Nineteen and all grown up, Laurie has decided to come and live with her father. Johnny is pleased to have her in town and asks her to stay at his apartment, but there is one problem—Laurie's jerky boyfriend Justin.

Although he tries to be a friend instead of a father, Fever eventually has to lay down some rules, including one excluding Justin and Laurie from sharing the same bed. Justin gets fed up and decides to leave, giving Laurie an ultimatum. Torn between her father and her "old man," Laurie chooses Justin.

Trivia: There's a picture of Fever with Mick Jagger on Fever's apartment wall, possibly serving as a reminder of the Doctor's previous success. Also, this was one of the few episodes in which Johnny willingly played a hit record—in this case, "The Long Run," by the Eagles.

Additional Cast

Laurie Caravella   Patrie Allen
Justin   Derrel Maury
Salesman   Milt Overman

Episode 0042
"Venus Rising"
Written by Steve Marshall & Dan Guntzelman
Directed by Nicholas Stamos

Venus is flattered by and interested in the $35,000 Program Director offer from rival station WREQ. Instead of being happy for their pal, the rest of the staff tries to figure out how to keep Venus from leaving. When Carlson and Andy talk about giving Venus a raise, Herb gets a great idea of his own—hoping to get a raise for himself, he decides to spread the word he has been offered a job at Channel 71 TV. The scheme backfires, however, and everyone on the staff simply congratulates Herb on his move.

Meanwhile, Venus finds out that WREQ, an automated station, just wants him for his color. He turns the offer down. Back at the station, Herb confesses his lie to Venus. Saying that he cannot tell Andy or Carlson about it, Herb cleans out his desk and leaves.

Andy, not knowing that Venus has turned down WREQ, comes in to offer Venus a $2,700 raise. Venus says he will take it—on one condition; Andy must offer $1,000 of that money to Herb. Dumbfounded, Andy agrees.

Great moment: When Herb wants to spread the word around about his new job, he naturally turns to Les, the station blabber-mouth. "Don't tell anyone," says Herb. "And Les—don't tell them soon."

Additional Cast

Jason Realli   Terry Kiser
Amanda Dean   Brenda Elder

Episode 0043
"In Concert"
Written by Steven Kampmann
Directed by Linda Day

Everyone at WKRP is excited about the upcoming Who concert, except for Carlson, who must take his son to the event. Fever, unable to find a date, agrees to go along with the Carlsons.

The next morning, Carlson, who ended up enjoying the show, enters in good spirits. He has a rude awakening, however, when the rest of the staff informs him that 11 kids died outside the concert, a tragedy eventually blamed on the problems of festival seating (general admission).

As the staff tries to make sense out of the senseless waste, Carlson begins to blame himself—after all, the station gave away tickets and promoted the event. Soon the staff begins to wonder whether Carlson will switch the station format back to elevator music. Carlson begins to feel better when he learns that Cincinnati plans to eliminate festival seating. "Aw, this is a great town," says Carlson. "We're responsible people here."

One of the series' most touching episodes, "In Concert" is almost like two separate shows. The first act, before the tragedy occurs, is played mostly for comedy. Particularly interesting is Carlson's cold-fighting aqua-mask, which Fever describes as "Disco bondage head gear." The second act—post tragedy—is a complete reversal, with heavy drama and pathos. The switch is so jarring that it actually reinforces the importance of the tragedy and made for an overall quality episode that handled the subject with great compassion and responsibility.

The final scene, underscored by Bill Evan's "After the Rain," is particularly powerful, with the following superimposed over the frame:

"On December 3, 1979, 11 people died outside of Riverfront Coliseum.

"On December 27, 1979, the City of Cincinnati passed an ordinance prohibiting 'festival seating' or general admission."

Episode 0044
"Filthy Pictures, Part I"
Episode 0045
"Filthy Pictures, Part II"
Written by Dan Guntzelman & Steve Marshall
Directed by Rod Daniel

When Carlson asks Jennifer and Andy to pose for a publicity photo for the Kiwanis Club's Charity Fashion Show and Bazaar, he has no idea of the trouble in store. The sleazy photographer—picked by Herb, of course—has taken candid nude photos of Jennifer while she was changing.

After several failed attempts at securing the illicit negatives—including one in which Herb must pretend he is gay to get the photos—Johnny finally comes up with a scam that works. Pretending that he is a men's magazine publisher, Fever, along with Bailey, cons the photos out of the photographer's greedy hands.

Additional Cast

Gonzer   George Wyner

Episode 0046
"Most Improved Station"
Written by Michael Fairman & Richard Sanders
Directed by Rod Daniel

Everyone is at each other's throat when WKRP loses the Cincinnati Broadcaster's Most Improved Station award. Les, who lost for best news personality, is particularly upset. It does not help matters any that Fever won for "Best Air Personality" and has let it go to his head.

Feeling the need to have everything out in the open, Andy calls a staff meeting. In the quasi-group encounter session that ensues, the staff, realizing that they are a family, finally resolves their differences.

This episode is a mother lode of psychological character development, particularly in the final scene. As with most WKRP episodes, the humor does not become a slave to the pathos. Indeed, in the final scene when the problems are resolved, Fever excuses himself, fearing an impending "group hug."

It is also very interesting to note that while Sanders had written the episode, his character was no more prominent than any of the others. When most sitcom stars write an episode for a show, it is usually one that primarily concerns their character. "Most Improved Station" was a refreshing change from that convention.

Additional Cast

Celeste   Colleen Kelly

The Third Season—1980-1981

Episode 0047
"The Airplane Show"
Written by Michael Fairman and Richard Sanders
Directed by Rod Daniel

Les has finally decided to take on the helicopter gap that exists between WKRP and WPIG. On the day before Veteran's day, as the PIG's "Eye in the Sky" copter reports traffic conditions, Les, in a bi-plane that he calls the "Fish Eye in the Sky," sweeps by the PIG copter and almost crashes into a bridge.

Carlson is furious with Les and grounds the newsman, forbidding him to even go to the bathroom without managerial approval. Frustrated, Les decides to go up once more on Veteran's Day. When the pilot, Buddy Barker, holds Les hostage until the people of Cincinnati hold a Veteran's Day Parade, Les begins to regret his decision. In a weird twist of events, however, the entire city of Cincinnati saves the newsman's life.

Additional Cast

Buddy Barker   Michael Fairman
Stunt Pilot   Harold Johnson

Episode 0048
"Jennifer Moves"
Written by Hugh Wilson
Directed by Rod Daniel

Jennifer soon begins to regret her decision to move into a $125,000 home in Landersville, Ohio. After just one day in her new home she has caused the break-up of one marriage, lost her piano, and had a run-in with the local suburban sex pervert. Wait, there is more—Les thinks that the house is haunted and a neighbor drops by to say that a new 14-story building is slated to be constructed at the end of the block. Welcome to the suburbs, Jennifer.

Trivia: Les had an aunt Eureka who once lived in a house just like Jennifer's. It seems Eureka filled the house with birds and eventually went crazy.

Additional Cast

Dottie Dahlquist	Judity-Marie Bergen
Ken Dahlquist	Terry Wills
Wayne Kraven	Ken Kimmins
Mr. Furgood	Dan Barrows
Policeman	Milt Traver
Elderly Woman	Georgia Schmidt

Episode 0049
"Real Families"
Written by Peter Torokvei
Directed by Rod Daniel

Cincinnati's own Herb Tarlek is the focus of an episode of "Real Families," the show that each week asks the question: "Hey America— Who are you—Really?" Despite the fact that the show has a reputation for digging up dirt on innocent people, Herb feels that he, his wife Lucille, daughter Bunny and son Little Herb can serve as an example of a clean living family. However, when hosts Phil Tarry and Elaine Parker show up with the film crew a day early the trouble begins, and Herb is painted as a liar and a bigot.

It is amazing that there can be this much humor in one half-hour; "Real Families" is perhaps *WKRP*'s finest episode. Edie McClurg is terrific as Mrs. Tarlek, seen here in a much more developed role than the one she played in "Goodbye Johnny." There's a lot of inside humor as well, including a little jab at *Little House on the Prairie*, *WKRP*'s chief competition during most of its four-year run.

Additional Cast

Phil Tarry	Peter Marshall
Elaine Parker	Daphne Maxwell
Lucille Tarlek	Edie McClurg
Bunny Tarlek	Stacy Heather Tolkin
Herb Tarlek, III	N.P. Schoch
Vargus Enswiller	Jim Hudson

Episode 0050
"Hotel Oceanview"
Written by Steven Kampmann
Directed by Rod Daniel

When Andy, Herb and Carlson go off to Dayton to try and win the Vicky Von Vickey Jeans account, the trio gets more than they bargained for. Herb almost falls for a transsexual, and Carlson thinks he is being pursued by the infamous Dayton Poisoner. Needless to say, they fail to win the account.

The best moments of this episode are those that involve Herb and Nicky Sinkler, the transsexual woman who, before her operation, used to be Herb's high school pal. Interestingly enough, Frank Bonner ended up in a similar character role in a 1990 episode of Carol Burnett's *Carol & Company*.

Special Guest Star

Vicky Von Vicky	Dr. Joyce Brothers

Additional Cast

Nicky Sinkler	Linda Carlson
Micky Broadhead	Larry Mankin

Episode 0051
"The Baby"
Written by Blake Hunter
Directed by Rod Daniel

Carmen Carlson is ready to deliver her baby. Arthur Carlson, on the other hand, is not looking forward to witnessing a natural childbirth. Having second thoughts, he roams around the hospital, seeking advice from the rest of the WKRP gang that has assembled for the happy occasion.

Additional Cast

Dr. Levin	Andy Romano
Receptionist	Edward Marshall
Nurse Smith	Jacque Lynn Colton
Peggy Sue	Dolores Albin
Candy Striper	Darian Mathias

Episode 0052
"Bah, Humbug"
Written by Lissa Levin
Directed by Rod Daniel

For its second Christmas episode, *WKRP* gives its version of "A Christmas Carol," with the stingy Carlson haunted by the three ghosts of Christmas.

Jennifer, the first ghost, takes Carlson back to December 24, 1954, where a squeaky voiced Arthur Carlson worked as a salesman for the station. Other older employees include Dan Bassett, "the meanest newsman who ever lived," Mrs. Butterworth, the old receptionist, Mr. Armor, the kind station manager, and a young Les Nessman with hair.

Venus acts as the Ghost of Christmas present, showing Carlson his disgruntled employees. Fever then takes Carlson into the not-too-distant future. Showing that the station has become automated, he reveals that Herb, who has taken to talking to himself, is the only employee left. Bailey now runs a TV station in Chicago, Andy breeds guard dogs in

New Mexico, Venus bought a clothing company called "Upwardly Mobile," and Jennifer got married and bought an island off the coast of Sardinia. Les Nessman became the Republican Whip of the U.S. Senate, and Fever just sort of "disappeared."

Upset by the horrors he has seen, Carlson gets out his check book and distributes bonuses to the staff.

A cute idea that is executed well, it is interesting to note that Hugh produced a similar Christmas show for *The Amazing Teddy Z*. Also, note the attention to continuity paid to the chronology of Carlson's tenure at WKRP. In "Mama's Review," Carlson said that he had been the manager of WKRP since 1955. In this episode he goes back to 1954, which, as the show reveals, was the year that Mr. Armor was fired (no doubt because he gave Christmas bonuses). There is a continuity problem with Les, however, because a 1982 episode says that the newsman had only worked at the station for 12 or 14 years.

Additional Cast

Mr. Armor	Parley Baer
Don Bassett	Don Diamond
Mrs. Butterworth	Marie Earle

Episode 0053
"A Mile in My Shoes"
Written by Dan Guntzelman
Directed by Rod Daniel

When Herb has to go on jury duty, Andy, thinking he will have an easy time at landing new sales and collecting on some long overdue accounts, decides to take over sales. Things do not go as well as planned—Even dressed in a sharp three-piece suit, Andy can't make a sale. He also gets hoodwinked by Smiling Al of Smiling Al's O.K. Coral RV's, an account that is $9,000 in debt.

Meanwhile, Herb, who was elected jury foreman, is having trouble getting the other eleven members to go along with his decision. Fever is not very pleased either—Venus has become Acting P.D. and wants Fever to play Urban Contemporary music.

When Herb returns, he is fooled by Andy's fancy attire and at first thinks that he has been replaced. Andy, having a newfound appreciation for Herb's job, welcomes the salesman with open arms.

Great moment: Les has just finished reading "Black Like Me," and he wants to dye himself black and do a series of reports based on the book. Andy says he likes the idea but tells the newsman to ask Venus, the Acting P.D., for final approval.

Additional Cast

Smiling Al	Nobel Willingham
Old Immigrant Man	Walter Janowitz
Young Lady	Jessica Nelson
Young Man	Joseph Reale

Episode 0054
"Baby, It's Cold Inside"
Written by Blake Hunter
Directed by Rod Daniel

The furnace has gone out at the Flem building, and Fever has resorted to other means of keeping warm—in violation of FCC rules, he is drinking on the air. Jennifer joins Fever for a sip and things go along rather nicely—until Momma shows up.

Momma is not in her typical evil mood—in fact, she is down right human, reflecting on her ex-husband Hank. She goes on to reveal that she used to work on the Broadway stage. Recounting to Jennifer how she met her husband, Momma says that Hank dropped by backstage one night and won her over with his Midwestern charm. She talks of how Hank was no good at business matters, and tells of how she stepped in to make the business a success. In the process, however, she alienated her husband, which she now seems to regret.

Soon, Lillian becomes drunk. She requests that Dr. Fever play a Gershwin tune. Lillian then goes to the bullpen, and sings "Someone To Watch Over Me" to the rest of the gang. When Arthur returns to the station, he and Momma go to the cemetery to pay their respects to Hank Carlson.

Additional Cast

Momma Carlson   Carol Bruce

Episode 0055
"The Painting"
Written by Steven Kampmann
Directed by Rod Daniel

In order to score brownie points with the Big Guy, Herb attended a charity auction at Carlson's church and spent $100 on a painting he did not even want. When Bailey falls in love with the piece, Herb gives it to her—that is, until he finds out that Carlson will buy it back from him for more money. Herb finally sells Bailey the painting, but when he learns that it was donated to the auction by the rich Mrs. Van Geesen, Herb buys the painting back for $500. Much to his dismay, Herb finds that the painting was done by the rich woman's son, who is in prison for selling qualudes and does a painting per day.

Episode 0056
"Daydreams"
Written by Peter Torokvei
Directed by Rod Daniel

Carlson is nervous about a speech he has to deliver to the Annual Ohio Broadcaster's Dinner. In order to feel more at ease with the speech, he decides to deliver it to the WKRP gang. As Carlson discusses the history of radio, each of the staff members find themselves dozing off, day-dreaming about the lives they wish they had led.

Episode 0057
"Frog Story"
Written by Bob Dolman
Directed by Rod Daniel

Herb has accidentally sprayed pink paint all over his daughter Bunny's frog Greenpeace. Arriving at the station with the slowly dying frog tucked away in a shoebox, Herb tries to enlist the aid of his fellow workers in reviving the frog. After the frog dies, Herb wonders how he will break the news to his daughter.

Although he tries to replace Greenpeace with a new frog, Herb gets a case of the guilts and decides to come clean with his daughter— describing himself as a "walking fau pax (sic)," he apologizes for the accident. After all is forgiven, Bunny warns the new frog to stay away from her father.

In an interesting sub-plot, we see the sardonic side of Les as he tries to capitalize on Fever's hypochondria. When Fever begins to complain of a cold, Les tries to convince the Doctor that it may actually be a more serious disease.

Additional Cast

Dr. Hunnisett	Kenneth Tigar
Bunny Tarlek	Stacy Heather Tolkin

Episode 0058
"Dr. Fever and Mr. Tide, Part I"
Episode 0059
"Dr. Fever and Mr. Tide, Part II"
Written by Steve Marshall
Directed by Rod Daniel

Fever has been asked to host a local television program called "Gotta' Dance." When the DJ finds out that the attractive producer Avis Dropkin expects Fever to spin disco, Fever tries to bow out. Told in no uncertain terms that the TV station will take legal action against Fever if he refuses to honor his contract, The Doctor invents a new character, Rip

Tide, a disco loving "TV guy" with the morals of a snake.

Trying to convince the rest of the crew that the Rip persona is just a scam, Johnny is soon taken over by the dominant Rip personality; he even begins going out at night dressed in the Ripper's outfits, making it with young girls.

When Herb and Andy try to get Johnny to do Rip on the air at WKRP, Fever falls off the deep end and begins to attack his second personality. As he struggles back and forth to regain his true identity, Fever decides to destroy Rip on the air. Asking for payola and coming onto young girls in the studio audience, Rip is fired from the show and Johnny regains his sanity.

Though a bit fantastic, everything in Fever's past seemed to point to the feasibility of an episode of this sort. Recall that Fever had gone through a number of on-air personas before arriving at Dr. Johnny Fever. He also had a struggle with auditory hallucinations in the episode "God talks to Johnny." Add this to his years of drug abuse and Fever makes a perfect target for a schizoid disorder. Hesseman played the role brilliantly and the scene in which he struggles for control is particularly powerful. Shooting both episodes in one week, Hesseman admitted that he was quite worn out by the physical activity in the episode, which may have actually contributed to the realism he offered the role.

Special Guest Star

Avis Dropkin   Mary Frann

Episode 0060
"Venus and the Man"
a/k/a "Venus Teaches the Atom"
Written by Hugh Wilson
Directed by Rod Daniel

Cora Isley, the station cleaning woman, asks Venus to have a talk with her son Arnold, a young black tough who is involved in a street gang and is considering dropping out of high school. Though Venus is more than happy to talk with Arnold, he is taken aback when Cora describes the young man as "Big, Tricky, and Bad!"

When Arnold offers Venus a $100 bill to get a new jacket, the DJ begins to realize that he has his work cut out for him. How can he convince a young man who's making a good deal of money scamming on the streets to develop a belief in the joy of education? Realizing that Arnold is a betting man, Venus makes the boy an offer—If Venus can teach Arnold about the atom in three minutes, Arnold will return to school.

Utilizing perhaps one of the most effective forms of education, Venus describes the atom by likening it to a story of three street gangs. When Arnold realizes that he has learned something, he keeps his word and agrees to finish school. When Cora returns to thank Venus for all he has done, Venus admits that he cannot say for sure whether Arnold will return to school after the end of the year. It is this touch of honesty, along with the ingenious teaching method, that makes this one of *WKRP*'s finest episodes.

Additional Cast

Arnold Isley	Kenny Long
Cora Isley	Veronica Redd

Episode 0061
"Ask Jennifer"
Written by Joyce Armor & Judy Neer
Directed by Linda Day

Dean the Dream, an afternoon DJ at WKRP, is leaving for law school, and Herb comes up with a great idea that he hopes will win the 3-4 p.m. time slot—A "Dear Abby" type advice show. After 169 days, Herb comes up with the perfect host—Arlene Allen, author of the book "You Be You and I'll Be Me." However, when Arlene proves to be an unstable wreck, it's up to Jennifer to step in at the last minute and save the show—and she becomes an instant hit.

Filling in until Herb can find a replacement, Jennifer gives cute, off-the-cuff advice to the Cincinnati listeners. When her campy advice ends up causing one of her listeners to be beaten by her husband, however, Jennifer decides to call it quits and Fever takes over the show.

Additional Cast

Arlene Allen	Eileen Barnett
Dr. Van Housen	Mickey Cherney
Herb's Cousin	Wayne Morton
Dancer	Feather Austin

Episode 0062
"I Am Woman"
Written by Lissa Levin
Directed by Linda Day

Bad news strikes WKRP—the Flem building is going to be torn down to make way for a new modern office building and the current tenants have three months to leave. When Bailey realizes that the Flem building, built in 1931, is an historic landmark, she decides to lead the "Save the Flem" campaign. Carlson is enthusiastic about it until Momma says that she will allow Carlson to build his dream building to house the radio station. Carlson tries to get Bailey to stop her crusade, but she defies his orders and continues with the cause. Upset, Carlson is ready to fire Bailey, until her eloquent speech against glass and steel box architecture wins the Big Guy back over to her side.

Episode 0063
"Secrets of Dayton Heights"
Written by Jon Smet
Directed by Frank Bonner

Les has been denied clearance to attend a Presidential press conference in Washington, D.C. because the secret service views Nessman as a security risk. Trying to get to the bottom of this, Andy, Carlson and Les go visit the local branch of the Secret Service. It is there where Les discovers his communist affiliation—it seems that Les' real father, Harvey Moorhouse, a barber in Dayton, Ohio, was once accused of being a communist spy.

This is all a shock to Les, who thought that his real father was Lester

Nessman, Sr. What had actually happened was Les' real father left before Les was born. Mrs. Nessman quickly remarried, but she let Les believe that Lester Nessman, Sr. was his real father.

Determined to see his father, Les goes to Moorehouse's barber shop in Dayton. Although it is rough going at first, Les begins to like the man. He never reveals that he is Mr. Moorehouse's son, but it is clear that Les will continue to visit Mr. Moorehouse.

This episode finally gave a reason for Les' hatred and paranoia of communism. We find that Mrs. Nessman had planted the seeds of the distrust when she told Les that all communists were "unreliable."

Additional Cast

Harvey Moorehouse	Bill McLean
Agent Berwick	Sam Anderson

Episode 0064
"Out to Lunch"
Story by Ben Elisco
Written by Peter Torokvei
Directed by Dolores Ferraro

Things seem to be looking up for Herb. After foundering in the world of insignificant clients and accounts, Herb believes he has a real chance at landing an account from a major ad agency. He begins having long, multi-martini lunches with the agency big-wig and soon begins forgetting about the clients he already has.

As Herb's drinking begins getting the best of him, things begin to fall apart. He has given away a $10,000 Irish Sweepstakes ticket and cannot even recall doing it. He loses the small client he had already landed. To add insult to injury, he finds out that the ad agency representative, a bigger drunk than Herb, was fired from the agency. Reviewing the problem with Carlson, Herb begins to realize that alcohol is not the sales tool that he thinks it is, but a crutch upon which he is growing dependent. With Carlson's subtle help, Herb decides to walk away from the bottle before it becomes a problem.

Gordon Jump's daughter has a bit role in this episode as the girl in the bar.

Additional Cast

Charlie Bathgate	Craig T. Nelson
Ray Margison	Michael Sherman
Girl in Bar	Cindy Jump
Bartender	Alan Toy

Episode 0065
"A Simple Little Wedding"
Written by Blake Hunter
Directed by Nicholas Stamos

In honor of their silver wedding anniversary, Arthur and Carmen Carlson decide to repeat their wedding vows. This is particularly important to the Carlsons, who had eloped during their first wedding to escape the big event that Momma Carlson was planning.

Deciding to just have a simple little wedding, they find things get more and more complicated. Herb throws the Big Guy an embarrassing bachelor party, and Momma, who convinced Carmen to allow a small shower, begins pressing for a big church wedding. Upset by the course the second wedding has taken, Carmen and Arthur end up eloping for a second time.

Additional Cast

Momma Carlson	Carol Bruce
Carmen Carlson	Allyn Ann McLerie
Hirsch	Ian Wolfe

Episode 0066
"Nothing to Fear But..."
Story by Tim Reid
Written by Dan Guntzelman
Directed by Asaad Kelada

When WKRP is broken into, the whole staff begins to get nervous. Giving into urban paranoia, Carlson decides to buy an expensive burglar alarm system. Herb, not a man to be caught uncovered, decides to buy a gun, which he keeps in his desk at the station.

Later that week, as the gang reluctantly goes off to Herb's unsuccessful client party on the first floor of the Flem building, Venus and Fever get suspicious when the alarm goes off at WKRP. With some trepidation, Venus agrees to get Herb's gun and together with Johnny, he searches the station. Feeling they have the burglar cornered in Carlson's office, the two find out it is only Andy, who has taken Stella, the hat check girl from the party, up to the station. It is a moment laden with tension as Venus holds the gun on a shaken and surprised Travis.

Additional Cast

Stella	Kelly Greer
Mailroom girl	Linda Rand
Intellectual	Robert O'Donnell

Episode 0067
"Til Debt Do Us Part"
Written by Howard Hesseman and Steven Kampmann
Directed by Frank Bonner

Johnny gets some great news—his ex-wife Paula is getting remarried. Tired of living off the "residue" of two ex-wives, Fever is elated. That is, until he meets the womanizing slob that Paula has decided to marry. Stuck between the idea of one less alimony check and not speaking out against Paula's fiance Buddy Gravers, Fever, who still seems to love Paula, tells her how he feels about Buddy. Paula says that she is still going to get married, but she seems to appreciate Johnny's concern.

Hamilton Camp, who played Buddy, was not the first choice for the role. Hesseman, who wrote the episode, recalled the problems he had in casting the episode: "Hamilton Camp was a replacement on Tuesday morning. I had written the show for Ruth Silveira and my friend the late John Matuzak, from the Raiders, who had done a feature with another *Committee* friend of mine, who wrote and directed it—it was called *Caveman* with Ringo Star. And he was looking to do a little TV, as well.

So I wrote this thing—I co-wrote it with Steven Kampmann—with John in mind. He came in on Monday and it was really disastrous, he—he just wasn't up to doing it. Sadly enough, I had to agree with everybody at the end of rehearsals on Monday that John wasn't really doing a good job—I had to agree that the best thing to do was cut and run, you know—cut him loose and bring in somebody else. And, I said, 'Hamilton,' and Hugh said, 'Exactly, that's what I was thinking' " (Hesseman).

Additional Cast

Paula	Ruth Silveira
Buddy Gravers	Hamilton Camp
Armenian Woman	Naomi Serotoff

Episode 0068
"Clean Up Radio Everywhere"
Written by Max Tash & Hugh Wilson
Directed by Linda Day

When a fundamentalist Christian group known as "Clean Up Radio Broadcasting—CURB" tries to edit WKRP's playlist, Carlson has to decide what is more important—religion or the First Amendment? After Johnny Fever proves that Dr. Bob Halyers, the Jerry Falwell-like character who runs CURB, wants to censor ideas as well as obscene lyrics, Carlson agrees to risk an economic boycott and fight CURB.

This episode is discussed in more detail in the chapter on the third season, but it is important to note that this last third season episode became an important turning point to the development of the rest of the series. Indeed, when Halyers got advertisers to boycott WKRP, the commercial free station began picking up great ratings. Later fourth season episodes expanded on this new found success, and the station was soon graced with a new lobby and, ultimately, more prestige.

Additional Cast

Dr. Bob Halyers	Richard Paul
Harvey Green	Ralph Manza

The Fourth Season—1981-1982

Episode 0069
"The Union"
Written by Blake Hunter
Directed by Linda Day

WKRP has climbed to tenth place in the Cincinnati market, but the staff does not feel that they are sharing in the station's success—they want more money. Invited to join the Brotherhood of Midwestern Radio Workers, Fever, Venus, and Bailey seriously consider it. When Carlson, who was planning on giving everyone raises, discovers that his staff is thinking of joining a union, he becomes upset. How could his "family" turn on him like this?

The resolution to this problem all turns on Andy, who has to walk a fine line between his affection for the workers and his responsibility to Mrs. Carlson. It seems that Andy has made a deal with Momma—he keeps the union out of the station and she pours more money into the place. By playing on their loyalties and emotions, Andy gets Carlson and the crew back together and the union is defeated by a vote of 5-4.

Additional Cast

Momma Carlson	Carol Bruce
Delivery Man	Robert Starr
Los Amigos Mariachis	Ray Sanchez
	Alberto Leyva
	Pedro Salas

Episode 0070
"An Explosive Affair, Part I"
Episode 0071
"An Explosive Affair, Part II"
Written by Steve Marshall
Directed by Linda Day

Joyce Armor, former WKRP receptionist, has returned to Cincinnati
to look up her old boss Arthur Carlson. Carlson begins to think that
Joyce wants to have an affair and he spends the better part of the episode
wondering whether he should go through with it. Meanwhile, the station
has received a bomb threat from a terrorist group known as Black
Monday, which last month blew up Channel 73 right in the middle of the
John Davidson Show. Just to be on the safe side, Andy has the station
evacuated and sends Fever and Venus out to the station transmitter to
keep WKRP on the air.

Out at the transmitter, Fever tries desperately to reach his bookie—
he just has to place a hunch bet on a horse named "Fever's Break."
Fever, unable to contact his bookie, loses control when he hears the
horse has won. Meanwhile, Andy learns that the bomb is out at the
transmitter and tries to call Fever and Venus, but to no avail—Fever,
angry at his bookie, has destroyed the phone.

Carlson, of course, has his own problems. Sitting in Joyce's hotel
room, he becomes uncomfortable with the idea of cheating on his wife.
When he finds out that Joyce only wants to talk with him about
becoming a client of her ad rep firm, Carlson begins to feel foolish.
Joyce makes Carlson feel better when she admits that she is flattered by
the misunderstanding.

Back at the station, Andy is going crazy trying to get a hold of his
DJs. A tense moment occurs when the signal goes dead and the gang at
the station fear the worse. Just when all hope is lost, Fever and Venus
return to the station—it seems Fever began to run off when he heard the
approaching sirens of the bomb squad; he thought they were the
telephone cops coming after him for destroying the phone.

Additional Cast

Joyce Armor	Rosemary Forsyth
Officer Madigan	Lou Richards

Episode 0072
"Rumors"
Written by Peter Torokvei
Directed by Linda Day

When Johnny stays with Bailey for a few days while his house is being fumigated for lizards, rumors start to fly that the two are having an affair. Even Andy and Venus participate in the off-color gossip and cat-calls. When Bailey finds out about this, she decides to put on a good show and make it look like she and Fever are sleeping together. Unfortunately, her plan backfires, and Johnny, who is depressed because he thinks Andy is trying to replace him with a younger man, starts to think that he has a chance with Bailey.

Additional Cast

Rex Erhardt   Sam Anderson

Episode 0073
"Straight from the Heart"
Written and Directed by Dan Guntzelman

While Herb tries to tell everyone that he is going away on vacation, Les is shocked to find out that the tacky salesman is going into the hospital for heart tests. About to depart for Omaha to receive the Agrarian Broadcasters Copper Cob Award, Les decides to visit Herb.

Not willing to give up on life, Herb leaves the hospital and he and Les go off to a see a 3-D porno film. Concerned about his best friend, Les calls the rest of the WKRP gang to join them at the theater to convince Herb to return for his tests. Before they can get anywhere, the place is raided and they all end up in jail. Thinking better of the situation, Herb decides to return for his tests.

Additional Cast

Nurse   Bonnie Urseth
Buzzy   John Brent

Episode 0074
"Who's On First?"
Written and Directed by Dan Guntzelman

In a continuation of "Straight from the Heart," Herb is upset to find that Andy has placed a want ad soliciting a new salesman. Carlson assures Herb that the appointment is just temporary, and, back at the station, the Big Guy gets mad at Andy for placing an ad that made it look like WKRP was looking for a permanent replacement. Determined to keep Herb's job open, Carlson agrees to take over for sales until Herb can return.

When Carlson and Jennifer go off to meet a concert promoter at a local stadium, Carlson is shocked to find out that Herb has arranged a kick-back scam with the promoter. To keep from ruining the deal—and to keep from looking like an idiot to Andy—Carlson poses as Herb and goes along with the sleazy promoter. That is not enough—the promoter wants to be sure that Carlson is as stupid as Herb has said he is and demands to go back to the station to meet him. Getting Les to pose as Carlson, Jennifer confuses the promoter enough to follow through on the deal.

Additional Cast

Pat Perillo	Dennis Lipscomb
Dave	Mickey Morton
Howard Liske	E. A. Sirianni
Nurse	Bonnie Urseth

Episode 0075
"Three Days of the Condo"
Written by Lissa Levin
Directed by Linda Day

Fever has finally come into a big chunk of money—$24,000 to be exact, the amount that was left from the $56,000 settlement Fever's attorney obtained from the L.A. station that fired the DJ for saying "booger" on the air. Not content to sit by and see his pal fritter away the money, Venus gets Johnny to invest in a condo from one of Herb's new clients, Gone with the Wind Estates.

Fever, not your average "condomaniac," ends up hating the place, but his landlords will not let him out of the deal. However, when Fever and Venus pose as homosexual lovers, the Gone-with-the-Winders are only too happy to see the DJ leave.

Additional Cast

Ms. Archer	Constance Pfeifer
Mr. Wainwright	Weldon Boyce Bleiler
Nadyne	Maryann Furman
Roberta	Denise McKenna

Episode 0076
"Jennifer and the Will"
Written by Blake Hunter
Directed by Dolores Ferraro

When Jennifer's 80-year-old companion Colonel Buchanan dies, Jennifer is named as the executrix of his will. The task is not an easy one, however, and Jennifer must fight against the Colonel's petty, greedy relatives. Things get particularly nasty when the family finds out that Buchanan has left the bulk of his estate to his buddies from the old "Fighting 42nd." Though the family promises to contest the will, Jennifer, who was only awarded one dollar of the estate, vows that she will honor the Colonel's last request.

Special Guest Star

Colonel Buchanan	Pat O'Brien

Additional Cast

Howerton	John Terry Bell
Andre	Roger Til
Chester	Brian Wood
Cloris	Janet Clark
Cedric	Ernie Brown
Skip	Charles Alvin Bell
Violinist	Shony Alex Braun

Episode 0077
"The Consultant"
Written by Hugh Wilson
Directed by Dolores Ferraro

With her bigger financial involvement in the station, Momma Carlson decides to spend more time protecting her investment and hires a consultant to monitor the station. Andy is furious when he finds out about this until he learns that the consultant is Norris Breeze, an old friend. When Norris turns out to be a coke snorting ingrate who threatens to give the station a bad report unless Andy buys his programming service, Andy realizes he has to take matters into his own hands.

By getting Carlson, Nessman and Tarlek to act like professionals— and getting the rest of the crew to act like they are out of their minds— Andy makes Norris' report on the station look ridiculous, much to Momma's dismay.

Additional Cast

Momma Carlson	Carol Bruce
Norris Breeze	David Clennon
Hirsch	Ian Wolfe

Episode 0078
"Love, Exciting and New"
Written by Lissa Levin
Directed by Frank Bonner

Andy has been seeing a lot of Momma Carlson lately—and not on just a business basis. He has taken her to dinner and to the opera. Venus thinks Andy is crazy, and Andy begins to think that he is becoming the victim of sexual harassment.

When Momma learns about Andy's suspicions, she decides to play it out to the hilt. Asking Andy to run away with her, Lillian scares the program director to death. Coming clean, Momma admits that she likes to be seen in the company of a younger man but that she is not interested in having a relationship.

During an interesting moment in the teaser, actress Colleen Camp plays herself being interviewed by Les.

Special Guest Star

Colleen Camp   as herself

Additional Cast

Momma Carlson   Carol Bruce
Hirsch   Ian Wolfe

Episode 0079
"You Can't Go out of Town Again"
Written by Dan Guntzelman
Directed by Howard Hesseman

Carlson is dreading his college reunion, and with good reason. His old college buddy Hank is a big blow-hard who is destined to ruin the affair. When Hank tells Arthur that Carmen only asked the Big Guy out as part of a sorority prank—Arthur was on the "dip list"—it is up to Carmen to convince Arthur that she really did end up falling in love with him at first sight.

Additional Cast

Hank   Claude E. Jones
Fluff   Joy Claussen
Jackie Winston   Rene Jones
Mrs. Hutchenson   Alice Nunn

Episode 0080
"Pills"
Written by Steve Marshall
Directed by Asaad Kelada

Herb has come across a lot of sleazy clients before, but Dave Wickerman is the lowest of the low. When Fever finds out that

Wickerman's diet pills are nothing more than over-the-counter speed, he refuses to voice the spots. By the time Carlson and Andy find out that Wickerman is pushing legal speed, it is too late—they have already agreed to run 18 spots per day for two weeks.

Ironically, if WKRP cancels the contract, they will be the ones in legal trouble. When Carlson learns that one of Wickerman's teenage clients collapsed from taking the diet pills, the Big Guy decides to risk the law suit and cancel the account. When Wickerman's landlord throws the sleazeball out, the gang at WKRP feel that they have won the fight. They later learn that Wickerman, who has the law on his side, merely relocated his business to the other side of town.

Additional Cast

Dave Wickerman   Robert Ridgely
Frank Bartman   Max Wright

Episode 0081
"Changes"
Written by Peter Torokvei
Directed by Will MacKenzie

Venus is worried when he has to face a reporter from a militant Black magazine; working around white people for so long, Venus feels that he has forgotten what Black life is all about.

Meanwhile, Herb faces an identity crisis of his own—out on a mercy date lunch with Jennifer, Herb decides that it may be time to change his wardrobe. When Herb and Jennifer return after lunch, the rest of the WKRP gang is shocked to find Herb decked out handsomely in a three-piece suit. However, the change backfires on Herb when his clothes put off one of his sleazy clients.

Back at the interview, Venus, who has changed into a more radical outfit, is surprised to find that the reporter from the magazine is white. Venus is further shocked to find that the reporter is working under the same sort of conditions as Venus. The moral of the story—do not pretend to be something you are not.

Tom Dreesen, who used to be Tim Reid's comedy partner, is

reunited with his friend in this episode, playing the role of the magazine reporter Rick Jesperson.

Additional Cast

Rick Jesperson	Tom Dreesen
Ted Jeffrey.	Art Metrano

Episode 0082
"Jennifer and Johnny's Charity"
Written by Blake Hunter
Directed by Will MacKenzie

When Johnny's friends at the Vine Street Mission lose their kitchen in a fire, Johnny decides to spearhead a campaign to raise the $40,000 needed to make the necessary repairs. Jennifer joins in the fight and, by inviting a few select people to a party at her house, promises Johnny she will provide the needed funds.

At the party, the two rich couples get carried away and decide to build the derelicts a new building out in the Price-Hill area, a fashionable Cincinnati suburb. Fever, who shows up at the party with a few of the Mission's "clients," is appalled at the idea—all the Mission needs is a kitchen, not a new building in the suburbs. As the rich folks begin to rub elbows with their benefactors, they soon learn the real meaning and purpose of charity.

Additional Cast

Charlie	Perry Cook
Judge Randall	Richard Derr
Percy	Carmen Filipi
Mrs. Mittenhoff	Helen Heigh
Shelia	Gloria LeRoy
Mr. Mittenhoff	John Vivyan
Mrs. Randall	Lynn Wood

Episode 0083
"I'll Take Romance"
Written by Lissa Levin
Directed by Asaad Kelada

Herb is desperate to try out the services of his new client, the I'll Take Romance dating service. In order to see if they are any good, Herb decides to submit his application under Les' name. Les, who has not had a date in two years, is a bit apprehensive, yet he agrees to give the computer date a try. When the girl turns out to be gorgeous, Les falls in love—that is, until Jennifer tells Les that the woman is really a hooker.

Les soon gets depressed, particularly since the hooker has called him up for another date. When Jennifer explains how that must mean that the lady really liked Les—no hooker would ever call a John for a date—the newscaster's spirits are buoyed.

Meanwhile, Andy, who has not had any luck lately in finding a date, decides to give the service a try. When he finds out that his perfect match is the same as Les', Andy gets suspicious. Les, aware of the situation, sits Andy down to explain the facts of life.

Additional Cast

Lorrayne Marvin   Livia Genise

Episode 0084
"Fire"
Written by Dan Guntzelman
Directed by Will MacKenzie

The Flem building is on fire and the WKRP staffers are stuck on the fourteenth floor. To make matters worse, Herb and Jennifer are stuck in the building's elevator. Though he begins to lose his cool at first, Herb finally pulls through when Jennifer begins to get scared. Even though he admits that he tells everyone he meets that he and Jennifer have sex on a regular basis, Jennifer develops a new respect for the tacky salesman.

Meanwhile, Johnny Fever has mounted a daring rescue attempt to save Jennifer and Herb. Coming through the trap door at the top of the stuck elevator, Johnny sees the two former rivals huddled in a close embrace. The fire out, Fever gets the elevator moving and all are safe.

Episode 0085
"Dear Liar"
Written by Steve Marshall
Directed by Frank Bonner

Les is upset because Andy wants to pull him off the newscaster's insightful report on vanishing vegetables and put him on a human interest story involving the Northside Children's Clinic. Not wanting to be bothered with the story, Les sends Bailey out to cover it.

After Bailey convinces the hospital director that a story on the center will do some good, Bailey is shocked to find the desperate conditions that some of the children are facing. Back at the station, Bailey comes up with an embellished story that could cost the station its license. Les, desperate to get Andy off his back, finds the story and reads it on the air—and lands the station in big trouble.

When the local newspaper wants to run a copy of the heart-wrenching story, Bailey comes clean and tells Andy that she made it all up. Not saying whether she would have changed the story even if she had the opportunity to broadcast it herself, Bailey offers her resignation. Andy refuses to accept it, saying that even though a woman was fired from the *Washington Post* for a similar incident involving an eight-year-old junkie, WKRP has a different form of journalistic integrity than the *Washington Post*.

Additional Cast

Edna Parkins	Barbara Cason
Clerk	Iona Morris
Doctor	Bill Ewing
Secretary	Susan McIver

Episode 0086
"Circumstantial Evidence"
Written by Tim Reid & Peter Torokvei
Directed by Frank Bonner

When a beautiful girl frames Venus as the ringleader of a burglary ring, the DJ must clear himself from the charges. When an eyewitness identifies a Black man with a beard as the culprit of a previous burglary, Venus has his work cut out for him.

After the judge rules that there is sufficient evidence to hold Venus over for trial, the detectives take Venus back to his cell in the county jail. On their way, they run into another man who has been arrested for burglary—the Black man bears a striking resemblance to Venus. The detectives realize the mistake they have made and Venus is freed.

Reid eventually married Daphne Maxwell, who played Jessica Langtree, the woman who framed him.

Additional Cast

Prosecutor	Robert Hooks
Judge	Jack Kruschen
Frank Bartman	Max Wright
Jessica Langtree	Daphne Maxwell
Detective Alcorn	Michael Pataki
Detective Davies	John Witherspoon

Episode 0087
"The Creation of Venus"
Written by Blake Hunter
Directed by Gordon Jump

When Momma catches Venus and Andy in some after hours horsing around at the station, the trio eventually begins discussing the truth behind the day Andy hired Venus. Via an inventive flashback sequence, we are transported back to the untold story that took place during the pilot.

As the episode unfolds, we find a disillusioned Andy trying to break the lease on his new Cincinnati apartment. When Gordon Sims, a full time teacher/part-time DJ from New Orleans, arrives, Andy decides to give the station one more try. Announcing that he is going to change the station's format to top-40 rock-and-roll the following day, Andy tries to build a new persona for Gordon—he decides to call him "Venus Rising."

After an interesting reprise of Fever's historic format change scene, we see how Venus reacted while he was waiting for Andy to finish convincing Momma to stick with the new format. It is during this scene that Andy introduces the new DJ as Venus Flytrap; Andy went on to claim that Mr. Flytrap had a great following down in New Orleans.

Back to the present time, Momma says that she was wise to the scam all along and proves it by rattling off some embarrassing histories of both Andy and Venus. After Momma departs, the two pals go back to their horseplay.

Additional Cast

Momma Carlson	Carol Bruce
Mrs. Murphy	Nora Boland

Episode 0088
"The Impossible Dream"
Written by Richard Sanders & Michael Fairman
Directed by Nick Stamos

Les, who is celebrating another birthday, is depressed because his career is going nowhere. In typical illogical Nessman fashion, Les decides to go to New York to audition for *The CBS Evening News*.

Jennifer plans a surprise birthday/going away part for Les, who arrives at Jennifer's early and ruins the surprise. When the rest of the gang arrives, Les decides to show the air-check video tape he had made for his trip to New York. After Les sees the tape, which is both comic and pathetic at the same time, he becomes even more depressed and leaves the party.

The next day, as the rest of the gang wonders whether Les left for New York, Mrs. Nessman (who looks exactly like Les) shows up at the station to blame the WKRP gang for putting this impossible dream in

194 America's Favorite Radio Station

Les' head. When Herb arrives, he thinks that Mrs. Nessman is Les dressed in drag; thinking his buddy has gone nuts, he "gooses" her. Almost immediately, Les enters, and Herb realizes the error he has made.

Additional Cast

Tiffany	Carol Carrington
Adele	Eleanor McCoy
Mrs. Nessman	Richard Sanders

Episode 0089
"To Err Is Human"
Written by Lissa Levin
Directed by Linda Day

Herb has done it again—this time he has messed up a very important account for a black hair care product. Where the promotional posters for the ad campaign were supposed to feature Venus Flytrap, Herb, in a terrible mistake with his printer, has wound up on the stand-up display himself. Carlson is so furious that he decides to finally fire Herb.

Jennifer, for some strange reason, is upset at the idea of Herb being fired. In order to save the salesman's job, she tells Herb to run over to the client and try to salvage the account. When Herb arrives, he discovers that the advertiser, Hester Sherman, is blind. Figuring that there is no way Mr. Sherman could realize how bad the stand-up displays look, Herb arrogantly tries to bluff his way out of the mess.

When Jennifer learns that Herb has made matters worse, she takes it upon herself to save Herb's job. Even though Mr. Sherman is blind, he can still sense the beauty of Jennifer Marlowe, and he decides to give WKRP one last chance.

Additional Cast

Hester Sherman	Tom Sullivan
Ms. Beeler	Sue Anne Gilfillin
Salesman	James Gallery

Episode 0090
"Up and Down the Dial"
Written by Dan Guntzelman
Directed by George Gaynes

WKRP has risen to sixth place in the Cincinnati market. While the gang is elated, their celebration is short-lived when Charles Von Sanker shows up to say that he is the new program director of WKRP—it seems that Momma is planning to change the station to an all-news format.

Though Momma promises that all current employees will have jobs with the new WKRP, the crew goes into a depressed tail-spin. A little bit drunk and a great deal angry, Johnny Fever arrives at Mrs. Carlson's home to have it out with the old lady. After Momma explains to Johnny the finer points of managing a complex business operation, Johnny realizes that Momma wants WKRP to lose money—that's why she's changing the format. When Carlson and Andy arrive at the house, Johnny threatens to tell Arthur Momma's real reason for the format change. Not wanting to disillusion her boy, Momma nixes the news idea and says that WKRP will remain as it is.

Additional Cast

Momma Carlson	Carol Bruce
Charles Von Sanker	Nicholas Hormann

Notes

[1]More detailed discussions of this topic can be found in the following sources:

Bagdikian, Benjiman. *The Media Monopoly*, Beacon Press, Boston, 1990. On page 114, Bagdikian speaks to the existence of an ABC pamphlet which stresses the importance of demographics.

Gitlin, Todd. *Inside Prime Time*, Pantheon, New York, 1985. See his chapter titled "The Turn Toward Relevance," pp. 203-20.

Taylor, Ella. *Prime Time Families*, University of California Press, Berkeley, California, 1989. See her chapter on "Prime Time Relevance," pp. 42-64.

[2]For a complete discussion of MTM and its quality programs, see Feuer, Jane; Kerr, Paul; Vahimagi, Tise. *MTM: Quality Television*, BFI Books, London, 1984.

[3]See a discussion of this and of other Falwell-like attempts at media influence in:

Powers, Ron. "The New Holy War Against Sex and Violence," TV Guide, 18 Apr. 1981, pp. 6-10.

It should be noted that the movement Powers discussed was not instigated by Falwell, but by Rev. Donald Wildmon, a Methodist minister who operated the National Federation for Decency. For more on this topic, refer to chapter 12 of Gitlin's *Inside Prime Time*, pp. 247-63.

[4]The Ron Powers article was published one week after "Clean Up Radio Everywhere" was aired. Powers made no mention of the episode in his article.

[5]According to Frank Bonner, Howard Hesseman had attended a fund raiser that was led by Ed Asner for the Sandinistas (Hesseman's attendance is documented in an article appearing in Variety,17 Feb. 1982, p. 94). Bonner cited this fact in his interview with me, stating, "*Lou Grant* and *KRP* were canceled at the same time—you can draw your own conclusions (Bonner)."

Furthermore, in his preface to *Inside Prime Time*, Gitlin also tries to tie in the cancellation of *WKRP* with *Lou Grant*. While this may have been the straw that broke the camel's back in the cancellation of these two shows, because *WKRP*'s time slots were shifted frequently before this event, it cannot be said to be the major cause for the series' demise.

[6]A "new" example of "biting-the-hand-that feeds" humor is evident in the *Simpsons*. The series *Moonlighting* served as an example of the type of show that "broke the fourth wall."

Works Cited

Interviews

Anderson, Loni. Interview with Author, 15 Oct. 1990, mechanical transcription.
Bonner, Frank. Interview with Author, 10 May 1989, taped transcription.
Chehak, Tom. Interview with Author, 29 Dec. 1989, taped transcription.
Hesseman, Howard. Interview with Author, 7 Jan. 1990, taped transcription.
Hunter, Blake. Interview with Author, 5 Jan. 1990, taped transcription.
Jump, Gordon. Interview with Author, 15 Feb. 1990, taped transcription.
Reid, Tim. Interview with Author, 4 May 1989, taped transcription.
Sanders, Richard. Interview with Author, 3 Jan. 1990, taped transcription.
Schanble, Chuck. Interview with Author, 31 July 1990, taped transcription.
Torokvei, Peter. Interview with Author, 1 Jan. 1990, taped transcription.
Wilson, Hugh. Interview with Author, 16 Jan. 1989, taped transcription.

Articles

Bedell, Sally. "TV Updates," *TV Guide*, 11 Nov. 1978.
"Biting the Hand," *Broadcasting*, 22 Jan. 1979.
"CBS Takes Light-Hearted Approach to '82-83 Sked," *Variety*, 12 May 1982.
Christensen, Mark. "Just Folks," *Rolling Stone*, 10 Mar. 1988.
"Close-Up," *TV Guide*, 26 Nov. 1979.
Davidson, Bill. "This is a Psychopathic Killer?," *TV Guide* 21 Oct. 1978.
Esterly, Glenn. "I Felt Ugly," *TV Guide*, 3 May 1980.
_____. "Being Himself Is Tougher Than Acting," *TV Guide*, 14 Feb. 1981.
Fong-Torres, Ben. "*WKRP in Cincinnati*: Real Radio on TV," *Rolling Stone*, 8 Mar. 1979.
Graham, Ellen. "How a Comedy for TV Overcomes Long Odds to Become New Series," *The Wall Street Journal*, Monday, 18 Sept. 1978.
Hano, Arnold. "You Can Call Him Johnny Fever or You Can Call Him Howard Hesseman or You Can Call Him Don Sturdy," *TV Guide*, 20 Oct. 1979.
"Headache in Hollywood—An Ailing Economy Takes Its Tool," *Broadcasting*, 21 Dec. 1981.
Hoover, Eleanor; Riley, Sue. "Howard Hesseman Puts The Spin and Loni Anderson A Hint Of Sin In *WKRP in Cincinnati*—And It Works Swimmingly, *People*, 12 Nov. 1969.
Knight, Bob. "Strike Hampers Semester Start," *Variety*, 30 July 1980.
Mahoney, William. "'MTM to Resurrect 'WKRP'," *Electronic Media*, 12 Mar. 1990.

198 America's Favorite Radio Station

"Meet the new 'WKRP Family'," *The Cincinnati Post*, 18 Sept. 1978.

Murphy, Mary. "Frank Bonner's Drive Can Be Tough on Him—and Others," *TV Guide*, 26 June 1982.

"People Cancelled, 'WKRP' on Hold," *Variety*, 15 Nov. 1978.

Powers, Ron. "The New Holy War Against Sex and Violence," *TV Guide*, 18 Apr. 1981.

"Reviews of New Network Series," *Variety*, 20 Sept. 1978.

"Six Faces of Youth," *Newsweek*, 21 Mar. 1966.

Stuart, Reginald. "Cincinnati Officials Order Inquiry Into Concert Crash That Killed 11," *New York Times*, 5 Dec. 1979.

Torgerson, Ellen. "I Would Never Do a Dumb Blonde," *TV Guide*, 17 Feb. 1979.

Tusher, Will. "Actor's Strike Halts Production," *Variety*, 23 July 1980.

Books

Alley, Robert S.; Brown, Irby B. *Love is All Around*, Delta Books, New York, 1989.

Bagdikian, Benjiman. *The Media Monopoly*, Beacon P, Boston, 1990.

Bedell, Sally. *Up the Tube*, Viking P, New York, 1981.

Brooks, Tim; Marsh, Earle. *The Complete Directory to Prime Time TV Shows, 1946-Present*, Ballentine, New York, 1979.

Cox, Stephen. *The Beverly Hillbillies*, Contemporary Books, Chicago, 1988.

Feuer, Jane; Kerr, Paul; Vahimagi, Tise. *MTM: Quality Television*, BFI Books, London, 1984.

Gitlin, Todd. *Inside Prime Time*, Pantheon, New York, 1985.

Kelly, Katie. *My Prime Time*, Seaview Books, New York, 1980.

McCrohan, Donna. *Archie & Edith, Mike & Gloria: The Tumultuous History of All in the Family*, Workman Publishing, New York, 1987.

Parish, James Robert; Terrance, Vincent. *Actor's Television Credits*, Supplement III, Scarecrow P, Metuchen, NJ, 1986.

Terrance, Vincent. *The Complete Encyclopedia of Television: 1947-1984*, New York Zoetrope, New York, 1985.

Winship, Michael. *Television*, Random House, New York, 1988.

Episodes

Armor, Joyce; Neer, Judy. "Bailey's Show," *WKRP* episode, MTM, 1978.

Dial, Bill. "Baby, If You've Ever Wondered," *WKRP* episode, MTM, 1979.

_____. "Turkeys Away," *WKRP* episode, MTM, 1978.

Guntzelman, Dan. "Up and Down the Dial," *WKRP* episode, MTM, 1981.

Hunter, Blake. "The Union," *WKRP* episode, MTM, 1980.

Magquire, Mary. "For Love or Money, Part I," WKRP episode, MTM, 1979.

Marshall, Steve; Guntzelman, Dan. "Venus Rising," *WKRP* episode, MTM, 1980.

Sanders, Richard; Fairman, Michael. "Most Improved Station," *WKRP* episode, MTM, 1980.

Torokvei, Peter. "Real Families," *WKRP* episode, MTM, 1980.

Wilson, Hugh. "Hoolum Rock," *WKRP* episode, MTM, 1978.

_____. "Les on a Ledge," *WKRP* episode, MTM, 1978.

_____. "Pilot, Part I," *WKRP* episode, MTM, 1978.

_____. "Venus and the Man," *WKRP* episode, MTM, 1981.

Unpublished

Ratings data provided by Nielsen Media Research, 13 Mar. 1990.

"WKRP in Cincinnati—Episode Numbers and Titles, Story Lines, Casts," Victory Television, New York.

Appendix A

Episodes Arranged by Writers

Note: "Written by" refers to the script, where "story by" refers to the concept or idea of the episode. Many episodes were written by more than one writer; when "with" appears below a title, it should be assumed that the writers shared equal credit for the script.

This list is arranged in the order by which the writers obtained their first credited script.

Written by Hugh Wilson
0001 Pilot
0002 Pilot, Part II
0004 Hoodlum Rock
0005 Les on a Ledge
0012 I Want to Keep My Baby
0013 Fish Story
  (Written by Hugh Wilson
  as Raoul Plager)
0015 Mama's Review
0018 Young Master Carlson
  (With Blake Hunter)
0023 Baseball
0032 God Talks to Johnny
0048 Jennifer Moves
0060 Venus and the Man
0068 Clean Up Radio Everywhere
  (With Max Tash)
0077 The Consultant
  (Story by Hugh Wilson)
0039 The Americanization of Ivan

**Written by Steve Marshall &
Dan Guntzelman**
0044 Filthy Pictures, Part I
0045 Filthy Pictures, Part II

Written by Bill Dial
0003 Preacher
0008 Turkey's Away
0011 Love Returns
0019 Never Leave Me Lucille
0030 Baby, If You've Ever
  Wondered

Written by Joyce Armor & Judy Neer
0006 Bailey's Show
0061 Ask Jennifer

Written by Tom Chehak
0007 Hold Up
0021 I Do, I Do...For Now
0022 Who is Gordon Sims?

Written by Blake Hunter
0009 Goodbye Johnny
0010 Johnny Comes Back
0017 Tornado
0018 Young Master Carlson
  (With Hugh Wilson)
0029 Put Up or Shut Up
  (With Steve Marshall &
  Steven Kampmann)
0031 Patter of Little Feet
0051 The Baby
0054 Baby, it's Cold Inside
0065 A Simple Little Wedding

0069 The Union
0076 Jennifer & The Will
0082 Jennifer & Johnny's Charity
0087 The Creation of Venus

Written by **Casey Piotrowski**
0014 The Contest Nobody Could Win

Written by **Richard Sanders &
   Michael Fairman**
0016 A Date with Jennifer
0020 A Commercial Break
0046 Most Improved Station
0047 The Airplane Show
0088 The Impossible Dream

Written by **Paul Hunter**
0024 Jennifer Falls in Love

Written by **Jim Paddock**
0025 Carlson for President

Written by **Mary Maguire**
0026 For Love or Money, Part I
0027 For Love or Money, Part II

Written by **Gene Fournier &
   Tom Joachim**
0028 Bad Risk

Written by **Steven Kampmann**
0029 Put Up or Shut Up
   (With Blake Hunter &
   Steve Marshall)
0043 In Concert
0050 Hotel Oceanview
0055 The Painting
0067 Til Debt Do Us Part
   (With Howard Hesseman)

See also Steven Kampmann &
Peter Torokvei

Written by **Steven Kampmann &
   Peter Torokvei**
0038 Sparky
0040 Herb's Dad

Written by **Steve Marshall**
0029 Put Up or Shut Up
   (With Blake Hunter &
   Steven Kampmann)
0033 Bailey's Big Break
0035 Les' Groupie
   (Story by Paul Hunter)
0058 Dr. Fever & Mr. Tide, Part I
0059 Dr. Fever & Mr. Tide, Part II
0070 An Explosive Affair, Part I
0071 An Explosive Affair, Part II
0080 Pills
0085 Dear Liar

See also Steve Marshall &
Dan Guntzelman

Written by **Steve Marshall &
   Dan Guntzelman**
0037 Jennifer's Home for Christmas
0039 The Americanization of Ivan
   (Story by Hugh Wilson)
0042 Venus Rising
0044 Filthy Pictures, Part I
0045 Filthy Pictures, Part II
   (Story by Hugh Wilson)

Written by **Dan Guntzelman**
0034 Mike Fright
0053 A Mile in My Shoes
0066 Nothing to Fear
   (Story by Tim Reid)
0073 Straight From The Heart
0074 Who's On First?
0079 You Can't Go Out of Town Again
0084 Fire
0090 Up and Down The Dial

Appendix B

This list is arranged in order by which the director directed his or her first episode.

Jay Sandrich
0001 Pilot
Written by Hugh Wilson

Michael Zinberg
0002 Pilot, Part II
Written by Hugh Wilson

0003 Preacher
Written by Bill Dial

0004 Hoodlum Rock
Written by Hugh Wilson

0008 Turkey's Away
Written by Bill Dial

Asaad Kelada
0005 Les on a Ledge
Written by Hugh Wilson

0006 Bailey's Show
Written by Joyce Armor and Judie Neer

0007 Hold Up
Written by Tom Chehak

0009 Goodbye Johnny
Written by Blake Hunter

0010 Johnny Comes Back
Written by Blake Hunter

0011 Love Returns
Written by Bill Dial

0012 I Want to Keep my Baby
Written by Hugh Wilson

0014 The Contest Nobody Could Win
Written by Casey Piotrowski

0015 Mama's Review
Written by Hugh Wilson

0016 A Date with Jennifer
Written by Richard Sanders & Michael Fairman

0019 Never Leave Me Lucille
Written by Bill Dial

0066 Nothing to Fear
Story by Tim Reid
Written by Dan Guntzelman

0080 Pills
Written by Steve Marshall

0083 I'll Take Romance
Written by Lissa Levin

203

Will MacKenzie
0017 Tornado
Written by Blake Hunter

0018 Young Master Carlson
Written by Hugh Wilson &
Blake Hunter

0021 I Do, I Do...For Now
Written by Tom Chehak

0024 Jennifer Falls in Love
Written by Paul Hunter

0025 Carlson for President
Written by Jim Paddock

0026 For Love or Money, Part I
0027 For Love or Money, Part II
Written by Mary Maguire

0028 Bad Risk
Written by Gene Fournier &
Tom Joachim

0029 Put Up or Shut Up
Written by Blake Hunter,
Steve Marshall & Steven Kampmann

0032 God Talks to Johnny
Written by Hugh Wilson

0033 Bailey's Big Break
Written by Steve Marshall

0034 Mike Fright
Written by Dan Guntzelman

0081 Changes
Written by Peter Torokvei

0082 Jennifer & Johnny's Charity
Written by Blake Hunter

0084 Fire
Written by Dan Guntzelman

Rod Daniel
0020 A Commercial Break
Written by Richard Sanders &
Michael Fairman

0022 Who is Gordon Sims?
Written by Tom Chehak

0030 Baby, If You've Ever
    Wondered
Written by Bill Dial

0031 Patter of Little Feet
Written by Blake Hunter

0035 Les' Groupie
Story by Paul Hunter
Written by Steve Marshall

0036 A Family Affair
Written by Tim Reid

0037 Jennifer's Home for Christmas
Written by Dan Guntzelman &
Steve Marshall

0038 Sparky
Written by Peter Torokvei &
Steven Kampmann

0040 Herb's Dad
Written by Peter Torokvei &
Steven Kampmann

0044 Filthy Pictures, Part I
0045 Filthy Pictures, Part II
Story by Hugh Wilson
Written by Dan Guntzelman &
Steve Marshall

0046 Most Improved Station
Written by Richard Sanders &
Michael Fairman

0047 The Airplane Show
Written by Richard Sanders &
Michael Fairman

0048 Jennifer Moves
Written by Hugh Wilson

0049 Real Families
Written by Peter Torokvei

0050 Hotel Oceanview
Written by Steven Kampmann

0051 The Baby
Written by Blake Hunter

0052 Bah, Humbug
Written by Lissa Levin

0053 A Mile in My Shoes
Written by Dan Guntzelman

0054 Baby, It's Cold Inside
Written by Blake Hunter

0055 The Painting
Written by Steven Kampmann

0056 Daydreams
Written by Peter Torokvei

0057 Frog Story
Written by Bob Dolman

0058 Dr. Fever & Mr. Tide, Part I
0059 Dr. Fever & Mr. Tide, Part II
Written by Steve Marshall

0060 Venus and the Man
Written by Hugh Wilson

Hugh Wilson
0023 Baseball
Written by Hugh Wilson

0039 The Americanization of Ivan
Story by Hugh Wilson
Written by Steve Marshall &
Dan Guntzelman

Frank Bonner
0041 The Doctor's Daughter
Written by Lissa Levin

0063 Secrets of Dayton Heights
Written by Jon Smet

0067 Til Debt Do Us Part
Written by Howard Hesseman &
Steven Kampmann

0078 Love, Exciting & New
Written by Lissa Levin

0085 Dear Liar
Written by Steve Marshall

0086 Circumstantial Evidence
Written by Tim Reid &
Peter Torokvei

Nicholas Stamos
0042 Venus Rising
Written by Steve Marshall &
Dan Guntzelman

0065 A Simple Little Wedding
Written by Blake Hunter

0088 The Impossible Dream
Written by Richard Sanders &
Michael Fairman

Linda Day
0043 In Concert
Written by Steven Kampmann

0061 Ask Jennifer
Written by Joyce Armor &
Judy Neer

0062 I Am Woman
Written by Lissa Levin

0068 Clean Up Radio Everywhere
Written by Hugh Wilson &
Max Tash

0069 The Union
Written by Blake Hunter

0070 An Explosive Affair, Part I
0071 An Explosive Affair, Part II
Written by Steve Marshall

0072 Rumors
Written by Peter Torokvei

0075 Three Days of the Condo
Written by Lissa Levin

0089 To Err is Human
Written by Lissa Levin

Dolores Ferraro
0064 Out To Lunch
Story by Ben Elisco
Written by Peter Torokvei

0076 Jennifer & The Will
Written by Blake Hunter

0077 The Consultant
Written by Hugh Wilson

Dan Guntzelman
0073 Straight From The Heart
Written by Dan Guntzelman

0074 Who's On First?
Written by Dan Guntzelman

Howard Hesseman
0079 You Can't Go Out of Town
  Again
Written by Dan Guntzelman

Gordon Jump
0087 The Creation of Venus
Written by Blake Hunter

George Gaynes
0090 Up and Down The Dial
Written by Dan Guntzelman